VETERANS APPEALS GUIDEBOOK

Representing Veterans in the U.S. Court of Appeals for Veterans Claims

RON SMITH, EDITOR

ABA
SECTION OF
ADMINISTRATIVE LAW
AND REGULATORY
PRACTICE

Cover by Tamara Kowalski/ABA Publishing.

Printed in the United States of America
17 16 15 14 13 5 4 3 2 1

Library of Congress Cataloging-in-Publication Data

Smith, Ronald L. (Lawyer)
Veterans appeals guidebook / edited by Ronald L. Smith.—First edition.
pages cm
Includes bibliographical references and index.
ISBN 978-1-61438-960-6 (print : alk. paper)
1. United States. Court of Appeals for Veterans Claims. 2. Veterans—Legal status, laws, etc.—United States. 3. Appellate procedure—United States. I. Title.
KF7713.S65 2013
343.73'0110269—dc23

2013007204

Contents

About the Authors

Anita Bhushan is an associate in Finnegan, Henderson, Farabow, Garrett & Dunner, LLP's Electrical practice group. Her practice includes litigation, client counseling, and patent prosecution with a focus on the electrical and computer technologies.

Elizabeth Ferrill is an associate in Finnegan, Henderson, Farabow, Garrett & Dunner, LLP's Electrical practice group. Her practice includes patent litigation in the electrical and mechanical fields and design patent prosecution.

Stephen Hennessy is an attorney in Finnegan, Henderson, Farabow, Garrett & Dunner, LLP's IP Specialties practice group. His practice focuses on patent litigation and patent prosecution with a concentration in materials sciences and business method patents.

Maureen Queler is an associate in the Finnegan, Henderson, Farabow, Garrett & Dunner, LLP's Chemical practice group. Her practice focuses on Abbreviated New Drug Application (ANDA) litigation.

Ronald Smith is of counsel in Finnegan, Henderson, Farabow, Garrett & Dunner, LLP's IP Specialties practice group. His practice focuses exclusively on pro bono veterans matters. Mr. Smith has prosecuted more than 400 veterans appeals in the federal courts, including before the Court of Appeals for the Federal Circuit and the Court of Appeals for Veterans Claims.

Preface

This book seeks to assist practitioners representing veterans and other claimants who are appealing or wish to appeal to the United States Court of Appeals for Veterans Claims (CAVC). It addresses the basics of appeals to the CAVC, explores the jurisdiction of the court, and outlines the CAVC appellate process. Many practitioners either have not previously handled an appeal to the court or do so only infrequently. This book, we hope, will facilitate their appeals to the court and perhaps increase the chances for appellate success.

The CAVC hears appeals from adverse decisions of the Board of Veterans' Appeals (BVA or the Board).[1] The Board is part of the Department of Veterans Affairs (VA). The court is not part of the VA, but is an impartial Article I court. The court has as many as nine judges, appointed by the President and confirmed by the Senate. Many appeals are decided by only one of these judges, but the court may sit as a panel of three judges, or the entire court may decide a case.

A veteran who decides to appeal a Board decision to the court is bringing a legal action against the Secretary of Veterans Affairs. Thus, the veteran is the appellant, and the Secretary is the appellee. The court's review of an appeal is an adversarial process, and the pro-veteran rules under which the VA decides claims do not generally apply to the court. Like all courts, the CAVC has specific Rules of Practice and Procedure that must be followed. An appeal or other matter can be dismissed or delayed if either party fails to follow these rules.

Disclaimer

We provide the material in this guide for information purposes only and do not render legal advice or provide a substitute for legal

1. http://www.uscourts.cavc.gov/about/how_to_appeal/.

counsel. The information found here may or may not reflect the most current legal developments or CAVC rules. Accordingly, practitioners must review current CAVC rules to identify changes the court may have adopted and conduct independent research to ensure that they are relying on the most recent case law. The current rules are available at http://www.uscourts.cavc.gov/court_procedures. The information in this guide is not promised or guaranteed to be correct or complete and should not be relied upon as such.

For convenience, this guide contains links to websites maintained by certain organizations and agencies. Neither the authors nor the publishers of this guide necessarily endorse, sponsor, or approve any third-party content that may be accessible in this manner and are not responsible for that content.

While we have attempted to provide information as accurately as possible based on the rules and procedures of the CAVC in effect at the time of publishing, the guide may contain errors or omissions, including those resulting from changes in the court's rules and procedures made after publication, for which we disclaim any liability. Readers should not take any actions, or refrain from taking any actions, based on information in this guide, without first consulting their own attorney(s).

Table of Authorities

Federal Cases

Federal Statutes

Federal Regulations

Federal Rules

CAVC Local Rules

CAVC E-Filing Rules

Other Authorities

Forms and Samples

PART 1

Introduction

I. Introduction to Representing Veterans Before the Court of Appeals for Veterans Claims

The United States Court of Appeals for Veterans Claims (CAVC) has exclusive jurisdiction to hear appeals from decisions by the Department of Veterans Affairs Board of Veterans' Appeals (the Board). Claimants for VA benefits start their claims at a VA Regional Office, generally located in the state where the claimant resides. Claimants who disagree with the findings of the Regional Office may appeal to the Board and eventually, if necessary, to the CAVC. The CAVC may not directly review a rating decision issued by a Regional Office.

The CAVC frequently hears appeals involving claims for service connection of a disability, increased disability ratings, compensation for medical malpractice, and compensation to the surviving spouse of a veteran who had a service-connected disability. Other less common claims include those for education or home loan benefits, specially adapted housing or adaptive equipment for cars, and waiver of overpayments made by the VA.

A. What Does It Mean to Be a "Veteran"?

Most claimants must be veterans. Colloquially, a veteran is someone who served on active duty in the Armed Forces of the United States.[1]

1. Active duty means full-time service, other than active duty for training or reserve service, as a member of the Army, Navy, Air Force, Marine Corps, or Coast Guard, or as a commissioned officer of the Public Health Service, Environmental Science Services Administration, or National Oceanic and Atmospheric Administration, or its predecessor, the Coast and Geodetic Survey. *See* 38 U.S.C. § 101(21).

For the purpose of determining whether a person is a veteran entitled to claim benefits from the VA, however, not everyone who served in the Armed Forces is a veteran. A successful claimant must generally be a former member of the Armed Forces who was discharged under conditions other than dishonorable. 38 C.F.R. § 3.1 (2011). In other words, those persons discharged under dishonorable or bad-conduct discharges may be barred from collecting VA benefits. Otherwise eligible veterans who are in prison may have their benefits reduced.

Others entitled to claim certain benefits include the veteran's spouse, dependent children, and, in some cases, dependent parents. The terms "veteran," "child," "surviving spouse," and "parent," among many others, are defined in 38 U.S.C. § 102.[2]

B. What Does It Mean to Be a "Disabled Veteran"?

Most appeals are filed by veterans who are disabled as a result of their military service. Many appeals arise as a result of VA decisions denying that a disability is "service connected." "Service connected" simply means that a disability or death resulted from an injury or disease, 38 U.S.C. § 1110, or the aggravation of an injury or disease, 38 U.S.C. § 1153, incurred in the line of duty during active, as opposed to reserve, military service. Other common appeals result from claims by veterans to whom the VA has already awarded service connection and who are seeking higher disability ratings.

C. To What Type of "Benefits" Might a Disabled Veteran Be Entitled?

The law provides many potential benefits for veterans, as well as dependents and survivors of veterans. A veteran may qualify for monthly, tax-free, monetary benefits, depending on the degree of the disability or disabilities and the number of a veteran's dependents. Veterans with certain severe disabilities may be eligible for additional

2. In the context of this book, the term "veteran" will be used, but also refers to these other types of petitioners, including a deceased veteran's spouse or dependent children.

special monthly compensation at rates that may exceed that paid for total disability. 38 U.S.C. § 1114(k)–(t). Also, the VA is required to provide medical care for all service-connected disabilities, including medications. If a veteran is 50 percent or more disabled, then the VA is required to provide the veteran with medical care for all conditions, whether or not service connected.

A surviving spouse, child, or parent may be entitled to Dependency and Indemnity Compensation (DIC). *See, e.g.*, 38 U.S.C. §§ 1311, 1313, 1315. DIC is a monthly cash payment.

A veteran permanently and totally disabled or the spouse or child of a veteran may also be entitled to educational assistance from the VA. *See, e.g.*, 38 U.S.C. § 3510.

D. Why Practice This Type of Law?

There are a number of reasons lawyers may be interested in appeals to the CAVC. First, helping veterans and their families may be personally rewarding. In addition, VA disability claims are somewhat similar to Social Security claims and may provide an opportunity to expand an existing practice. Moreover, this type of work can satisfy pro bono obligations, because many veterans and their families are economically disadvantaged. Finally, attorneys may earn fees from the VA under the Equal Access to Justice Act (EAJA), 28 U.S.C. § 2412, or from the veterans themselves.

E. Scope of CAVC Rules (Rule 1)[3]

The court has statutory authority to adopt its own rules known as Local Rules. 38 U.S.C. § 7264. Practice before the court is not governed by the Federal Rules of Appellate Procedure.

3. All Rules are references to the CAVC Local Rules (Vet. App. R.).

II. Some Common Types of Cases

A. Service Connection for a Disability

The VA recognizes two types of service connection: direct and by aggravation.

1. DIRECT SERVICE CONNECTION

Direct service connection is the more common type of service-connection claim. Direct service connection means that the veteran has a disability related to an injury or disease incurred during active duty military service. 38 U.S.C. § 1110. There are three elements that generally must be proven in order to establish direct service connection for a disability:

1. in-service incurrence of an injury or disease;
2. the existence of a present disability; and
3. a nexus between the injury or disease and the disability.

See Hickson v. West, 12 Vet. App. 247, 253 (1999).

2. SERVICE CONNECTION BY AGGRAVATION

Service connection by aggravation allows an injury or disease that preexisted the veteran's military service to be service connected. The veteran's preexisting disability must have been noted—that is, actually found as opposed to reported as history, 38 C.F.R. § 3.304 (2011)—on the report of the veteran's examination upon entering military service. Service connection based on in-service aggravation will be awarded when the record shows that the preexisting disability underwent a permanent increase in severity during service. *See* Beverly v. Brown, 9 Vet. App. 402, 405 (1996).

B. Increased Rating for a Disability Already Service Connected

When the VA grants service connection for a disability, it also determines a disability rating. There are eleven disability ratings, from 0 to 100 percent in 10-percent increments. 38 U.S.C. § 1114; 38 C.F.R.

§ 4.31 (2011) (establishing a 0-percent evaluation).[4] If the severity of a veteran's disability increases after the VA awards service connection, the veteran is entitled to claim a higher rating.

C. Medical Malpractice

If a veteran suffers disability, additional disability, or death as a result of VA hospital care, medical or surgical treatment, or examination, then that additional disability or death may be compensated as if it were service connected. 38 U.S.C. § 1151. The additional disability or death must have resulted from carelessness, negligence, lack of proper skill, error in judgment, or a similar instance of fault on the part of the VA, or the disability may have resulted from an event that was not reasonably foreseeable. Negligence may include the VA's failure to obtain the patient's full and informed consent to the treatment or procedure. *See* 38 U.S.C. § 7331; 38 C.F.R. §§ 3.361(d)(1)(ii), 17.32 (2011).

III. How a Claim Reaches the CAVC

A. Claims Begin at the Department of Veterans Affairs Regional Office

1. REGIONAL OFFICES

The VA has Regional Offices in most states as well as Puerto Rico, Guam, and the Philippines. A case begins when a person files a claim with one of these offices.[5]

The Regional Office initially decides the claim and, if it is granted, makes the initial decision identifying the disability and the appropriate rating for the VA. A veteran who is dissatisfied with the Regional

4. If a veteran is awarded a "0 percent" disability rating, then the veteran does not receive monetary disability benefits but may be entitled to medical care related to the disability at a VA facility. Two or more service-connected disabilities rated 0 percent disabling may entitle a veteran to a 10 percent rating. 38 C.F.R. § 3.324 (2011).

5. For the address of a Regional Office and directions, see http://www2.va.gov/guide/home.asp. This webpage lists Regional Offices as well as healthcare facilities and cemeteries. The general toll-free telephone number is (800) 827-1000.

Office's decision on a claim may initiate an administrative appeal to the Board by filing a Notice of Disagreement (NOD). To be timely, the NOD must be filed within one year following the date the claimant is notified of the decision being appealed. After filing the NOD, the veteran may additionally elect to have the decision reviewed at the Regional Office by a Decision Review Officer. This person is usually a senior adjudicator and has the authority to reverse or modify the original decision.

2. FILING A FORM 9

If the veteran does not elect review by the Decision Review Officer or continues to be unsatisfied with the result of that review, the veteran must file a written appeal, known as a Form 9, with the Regional Office.

3. FILING DEADLINE FOR FORM 9

There are three different ways to calculate how much time a claimant has to complete and file a Form 9. The applicable deadline for filing is the one that gives the veteran the most time to file the appeal.

- First, the veteran has *one year* from the day the Regional Office mailed the notice of the decision being appealed.
- Second, the veteran has *60 days* from the day the Regional Office mailed a Statement of the Case (SOC) to the veteran.[6]
- Finally, in some cases, the Regional Office may have mailed an update to the SOC, called a Supplemental Statement of the Case (SSOC), to the veteran. If that SSOC was provided in response to evidence submitted by or on behalf of the veteran, and the veteran had not already filed a Form 9, then the veteran has at least *60 days* from the date the Regional Office mailed the SSOC to file the Form 9, even though the one-year period has already expired. *See* 38 C.F.R. § 20.302(b)(2) (2011).

6. An SOC includes a summary of the evidence, citation to pertinent laws and regulations, and a decision on each issue along with a summary of the reasons for each decision. 38 U.S.C. § 7105(d)(1).

Once the Regional Office receives the Form 9, it sends the veteran's case to the Board.

B. From the Regional Office to the Board

1. STANDARD OF REVIEW

The Board's standard of review is de novo, meaning that the Board is not required to give any deference to the Regional Office's decision. The Board's jurisdiction, however, is appellate, so it reviews decisions made by the Regional Office but will not decide in the first instance issues not addressed by the Regional Office. 38 C.F.R. § 20.101(a) (2011). Board decisions are generally final as of the date stamped on the first page of the decision. *See* 38 C.F.R. § 20.1100 (2011).

2. ADDITIONAL EVIDENCE

Under some circumstances, the Board may direct that additional evidence be added to the record. 38 C.F.R. § 20.709 (2011).

3. HEARING BEFORE THE BOARD

After the Regional Office sends the case to the Board, the Board will hold a hearing, if one is requested. Moreover, the veteran is entitled to a hearing before the Board so long as the veteran or his or her representative appears. 38 C.F.R. § 20.700 (2011). A transcript of any hearing will be included in the veteran's VA file. 38 C.F.R. § 20.714 (2011).

C. Appealing a Board Decision to the CAVC

Veterans and other claimants have a statutory right to a CAVC review of a Board decision.

1. DEADLINE FOR FILING A NOTICE OF APPEAL

Any appeal from a Board decision must be filed no later than 120 days after the date stamped on the first page of the Board's decision. 38 U.S.C. § 7266(a). If the 120th day falls on a weekend or holiday, the Notice of Appeal is due *no later than the prior business day.* A Notice of Appeal to the CAVC filed in error with the VA is ineffective. 38 U.S.C. § 7266(a); Rule 4(a). However, the common law "mailbox rule" applies to a notice of appeal properly mailed to the CAVC. Rios v. Nicholson, 490 F.3d 928, 932–32 (Fed. Cir. 2007).

STOP Extensions of time to file a Notice of Appeal are not permitted.

---

2. EQUITABLE TOLLING

Equitable tolling, however, is available in some circumstances. Bove v. Shinseki, 25 Vet. App. 136, 143 (2011).

Checklist for Filing an Appeal. An appeal to the CAVC is possible if the answer to all of the following questions is YES:

- ☑ Did the client receive a decision by the Regional Office?
- ☑ Did the client file an NOD with the Regional Office within one year following service of the Regional Office's decision?
- ☑ Did the client timely file a VA Form 9?
- ☑ Has the Board issued its decision?
- ☑ Was the Board's decision made within the last 120 days?

PART 2

Practicing Before the CAVC

I. Qualification to Practice Before the CAVC

Before attorneys may begin the task of representing veterans or other appellants in an appeal before the CAVC, they must obtain admission to the court's bar or file for permission to appear in the particular case. Rule 46(b)(1)(F). In addition, they must complete the mandatory training and registration in order to be able to electronically file papers with the court. The following sections review the rules governing admission and the key steps in that process. This section also briefly touches on the ability of nonattorney practitioners and law students to practice and appear before the court, as these practitioners may be of valuable assistance to attorneys handling appeals for multiple veterans.

A. Admission to the Court (Rule 46)

Rule 46 of the Rules of Practice and Procedure governs the process of becoming admitted to practice before the CAVC. Attorneys as well as nonattorneys and law students are all eligible to practice before the CAVC. However, the nonattorneys must be under the direct supervision of an attorney admitted to the CAVC bar. The following section details the steps attorneys must take to become admitted to the CAVC bar.

1. ATTORNEY ADMISSION

In addition to Rule 46 of the Rules of Practice and Procedure, there are also separate Rules of Admission and Practice, specifically, Rule 3, which supplements Rule 46 with regard to admission to the court's bar. Rule 3, which will not be discussed in detail here, should be consulted in cases of contested admissions, when an applicant may not be qualified for admission.[1]

Certificate of Good Standing. Under Rule 46, an attorney is a person "who has been admitted to practice in the Supreme Court of the United States, or the highest court of any state, the District of Columbia or a United States territory or commonwealth." If admission to one of the above courts has not been granted, then the guidelines for "Non-attorney Admission" should be followed, as explained below.

Initially, an attorney looking to be admitted to the bar of the CAVC should contact the highest court of the state in which the attorney is barred to obtain a certificate of good standing. In many states, this entails contacting the Supreme Court of the state. A web search for "certificate of good standing + state name" will often find state courts' websites that provide instructions on how to obtain this certificate. If an attorney is admitted to more than one state bar, only one certificate from one state is required for admission.

A certificate of good standing from the Supreme Court of your state is different from a certificate of good standing from your state bar organization—this certificate, which is required by the CAVC, must come from a state court, not the state bar.

If you have a spare certificate, it is crucial to check its date. The CAVC will accept only certificates issued within the three months before the filing date on the admissions application. Therefore, once a certificate is received from the state court, an attorney has at most three months in which to complete and file an application for admission with the CAVC for that certificate to be valid.

1. Copies of both of these sets of Rules can be found on the court's website at http://www.uscourts.cavc.gov, under "Court Rules and Procedures."

a. Application Form

The application for admission to the bar can be found on the CAVC website under the "Court Forms" tab and must be filled out completely. The application does not need to be notarized.

The last part of the application for admission is the "Motion" section. Admission to the CAVC bar must be made by a motion by a member of the court's bar. If the applicant does not know a member to move for admission, that section can be left blank, and a court staff attorney will make the motion for the applicant upon approval of the application.

YIELD

You must provide a personal phone number on your application form; failure to include this information will delay your admission.

After the applicant finalizes the application, it, along with the certificate of good standing and the fee for admission, should be mailed to the Admissions Clerk. As of 2012, the fee is $100.00 and can be paid by check or money order. The current fee and mailing address can be found on the application form.

2. NONATTORNEY ADMISSION AND APPEARANCE (RULE 46)

a. Nonattorney Practitioner

A nonattorney of good moral character and repute may be admitted to the bar of the CAVC. The nonattorney must at all times be under the direct supervision of an attorney, including during oral arguments. The supervising attorney must be admitted to the court's bar. In addition, each Notice of Appearance and pleading filed by a nonattorney practitioner must include the name, address, and signature of the responsible supervising attorney. There is a separate application form for nonattorney practitioners on the court's website under "Court Forms." The form is largely similar to the form for attorneys (see above), but this form requires a motion from the supervising attorney. The court's current application fee and mailing address can be found on the application form.

b. Law Students

Law students who are not admitted and nonattorney practitioners may appear in the court, participate in the preparation of briefs and other documents, and participate in oral argument before the court. The assistance of law students can help an admitted attorney with his or her workload, but supervision and knowledge of the case by the admitted attorney is still required.

Briefs and documents filed in the court must still be signed by the attorney of record in the case. The attorney of record must also assume professional responsibility for the law student's work, including timeliness, and for supervising the quality of the work. The supervising attorney is responsible for being familiar with the case and must be prepared to assist or correct the student's written or oral statements.

In order to appear in court, law students must be enrolled in a law school approved by the American Bar Association, have completed at least four semesters of study, be certified by the dean of the law school, be introduced by the attorney of record in the case, and certify in writing that they are familiar with the code of professional responsibility of the state in which their law school is located and the rules governing practice before the CAVC. Details of these conditions for appearance can be found in Rule 46(b)(1)(G).

The law student must also have the written consent of the veteran and the attorney of record.

3. REPRESENTATION REQUIREMENTS

After being admitted to the bar as either an attorney or nonattorney, or permitted by the court to practice without admission,[2] you must file a written Notice of Appearance to represent a party in any case before the court.

---

2. Under Rule 46(b)(1)(F), on motion and showing of good cause, the court may permit any attorney or nonattorney practitioner who is not admitted to practice before the CAVC to appear in a particular case.

a. Withdrawal (Rule 46(c))

A practitioner may withdraw representation when another practitioner has entered an appearance on behalf of a veteran in a case. In that situation, the withdrawing practitioner must simply file a notice with the court stating that the veteran has consented to the withdrawal.

The CAVC has adopted the ABA Model Rules of Professional Conduct.

In a situation where it is necessary to withdraw from representing a veteran and another practitioner has not previously entered an appearance on behalf of the veteran, the attorney must file a motion to withdraw. Details regarding the motion to withdraw can be found in Rule 46(c). Even if a motion to withdraw has been filed, the attorney's duty to the veteran continues until the court grants the motion.

Be sure that any motion to withdraw includes the veteran's telephone number. Rule 46(c)(1)(B).

B. Filing and Reviewing Documents in the CAVC

Effective October 14, 2008, the CAVC adopted an electronic filing system called Case Management/Electronic Case Files (CM/ECF). The use of this e-filing system is now mandatory for all represented parties unless granted an exception.[3] Accordingly, it is necessary for admitted practitioners to register for e-filing and learn how to use the CM/ECF system effectively for filing documents with the court. The court has

3. Self-represented parties may not electronically file without first obtaining court approval. Upon motion and a showing of good cause, the court may exempt a representative from the requirement to file electronically and authorize filing by means other than use of the CM/ECF system. An "E-Filing User Exemption" Form can be found on the court's website under "Court Forms." *See* E-Rule 3(b).

adopted E-Rules, governing the electronic filing of documents in cases before the court.[4]

To obtain access to the CM/ECF system, you must be admitted to the court's bar, as detailed above. Once you have completed the admission process, you may register with the court's CM/ECF system. *See* E-Rule 3(a).

1. ACCESS TO THE CM/ECF SYSTEM

To access the court's CM/ECF system, a practitioner needs a log-in and password, which are supplied by the court. You cannot file through CM/ECF without first registering and having the court approve you as an e-filing user.

a. Online Training

The first step in registering for e-filing is to complete the court's online training. This training can be accessed through the court's website at http://www.uscourts.cavc.gov, choosing the "Electronic Filing" tab, and clicking on "Training Modules." The training modules can be either viewed as a presentation or read as a PDF file.[5] Regardless of the form of the training (audio-visual presentation or PDF), it is mandatory for all applicants to complete the posted training modules before submitting the registration form.

Some e-filing tips from the training modules:

- A PDF Writer is required for e-filing (scanned documents are not accepted); exceptions to this rule include the client's signed retainer agreement and a Declaration of Financial Hardship.
- When accessing the CM/ECF system and selecting the log-in option, two windows will appear. These windows must both remain open in order to use the system. Closing the GRAY Application Window will exit the system.
- When filing a Notice of Appearance, it is critical to select the "Add Attorney" button after finding the attorney's name.

4. A copy of the E-Rules can be found at http://www.uscourts.cavc.gov/electronic_filing/EFilingRules.html.

5. In this context, a PDF is a file that is created using the Adobe Acrobat program and made to be viewed using the Adobe Reader program.

b. CM/ECF Registration Form

After completing the training, you must fill out the CM/ECF Registration form. This form is available on the court's website under "Court Forms" and "E-Filing User Registration." Fill it out, save it as a PDF file, and then e-mail it to efiling@uscourts.cavc.gov. All fields of the form are mandatory, and the applicant's electronic signature must be included on the form. More information about electronic signatures can be found in the section on "Filing Documents Using the CM/ECF System." In addition, an applicant must have and maintain an e-mail address and update the court regarding any changes in that e-mail address. There is no fee connected with registering to use the e-filing system.

c. User Name and Password Generation

Once the registration form has been e-mailed to the court, the system will generate the filing user's user name and password within a few hours to two days. When registration is completed, an e-mail will be sent from the court confirming the registration. The password can be changed in the CM/ECF system by accessing the "Utilities" menu. If a situation arises wherein a practitioner needs to file immediately before registration is complete, contact the Clerk of Court's office for instructions.

User names and passwords will arrive in separate e-mails from the court. The user name and passwords are both case sensitive. It is a good idea to keep these e-mails in a safe place for reference.

---

2. FILING DOCUMENTS USING THE CM/ECF SYSTEM

In addition to the training modules for using the CM/ECF system, the court has issued rules governing e-filing. They can be found on the court's website under "Electronic Filing" and "E-Filing Rules."

a. Type, Form, and Timing of Filings

All documents must be filed electronically using the CM/ECF system, except for documents initiating cases in the court (such as a Notice of Appeal or Petition for Extraordinary Relief, Notice of Appearance, and retainer agreement). Those documents may be filed electronically by attaching them to an e-mail sent to esubmission@uscourts.cavc.gov or by using conventional methods of filing. *See* Rule 25.

CAVC rules expressly allow a Notice of Appearance, fee or retainer agreement, and/or Declaration of Financial Hardship to be filed by e-mail to esubmission@uscourts.cavc.gov, but only when submitted concurrently with a Notice of Appeal. Rule 25(b)(3).

Remove All Personal Identifiers. Before they are filed, all documents must have all personal identifiers redacted. *See* E-Rule 4(a). "Personal identifiers" include social security numbers, VA claims file numbers (sometimes referred to as C-files), dates of birth, financial account numbers, and names of minor children. *See* E-Rule 1(a)(10).

Using the CAVC Case Number. If the appeal has been docketed, it is important for documents filed to contain the correct CAVC case number in the caption.

Creating Your PDF Document. When a document is filed electronically, paper copies should not be filed unless the court requests them. All electronic documents must be filed in PDF format. *See* E-Rule 2(f). Everything in PDF must be made using a "print to PDF" or a PDF converter program from the original word-processing file. This enables the document to be searched and copied. A scanned document will not be acceptable.

Each document must be its own PDF file. For example, if a motion for leave to file an extension of time and a motion for extension need to be filed, they must be filed as two separate PDFs. However, you must combine all exhibits and attachments related to a pleading with that pleading into a single PDF file. If a PDF document consists of more than one attachment or exhibit, then the first page of the PDF should be a Table of Contents corresponding to the pagination of the PDF file. E-Rule 7.

Naming conventions for saving PDF files can be found on the court's website under "Electronic Filing," "E-Filing Checklist," and "PDF Document Considerations." File names should generally incorporate the CAVC case number.

When to File Your Document. Filing is permitted at all times, unless the system is unavailable. Any filings completed before midnight will be entered on the docket as of that date. If a technical failure prevents you from timely filing any document, you should seek immediate relief from the court by sending an e-mail to efiling@uscourts.cavc.gov. E-Rule 5(e).

b. Electronic Signature

According to the court's rules for e-filing, "[t]he term 'electronic signature' refers to an electronic symbol attached to or associated with an electronic document and executed or adopted with the intent to sign the document." E-Rule 1. The signature must be that of the electronic filer (i.e., the signature on the motion must be for the same person who is logged in and filing the document). A signed copy of the filed document must be maintained until the appellate process is completed in the case.

The e-signature should not be in any different location from where a signature would normally appear on the document. For CM/ECF filings, you should type "/s/," followed by the name of the e-filer, and underline both parts. The e-signature is also normally followed by the typed name and title of the signatory. For example:

<u>/s/ John S. Doe</u>
John S. Doe, Attorney

The e-signature ("/s/") alone is not a satisfactory electronic signature—the "/s/" must be adjacent to the typed name of the signer, and the name and authority of the signer should appear on a separate line.

Checklist for Filing a Document with the CM/ECF System:

- ☑ Is the document a PDF?
- ☑ Was the PDF made from a Word document and not by scanning?
- ☑ Are all attachments and exhibits included in a consolidated PDF with the main filing?
- ☑ Is more than one filing included in the same PDF? If so, create separate documents.
- ☑ Is all personal information redacted?
- ☑ Is the PDF named according to the court's naming conventions?
- ☑ Does the document contain the correct case number?
- ☑ Does the document follow Rule 32 of the Rules of Practice and Procedure for the form of the papers?
- ☑ Does the electronic signature line contain the "/s/" with the practitioner's typed name after it?
- ☑ Does the signature line in the document for the attorney match the user who is logged into the CM/ECF system and who is e-filing?

3. HOW TO FILE A PLEADING

Detailed instructions (including screen shots) on how to file can be found in the court's E-Filing Training Manuals. There is also an e-filing "Checklist" on the court's website under the "Electronic Filing" tab.

4. SERVICE OF PLEADING

Electronic transmission of docket activity constitutes notice and service of a document, and registration for the CM/ECF system constitutes consent to receive service through docket-activity e-mail. *See* E-Rules 3(d) and 6. Because the e-mailing of docket activity constitutes notice and service, you need not separately file, mail, or e-mail a Certificate of Service.

a. Monitoring the Docket

In addition to allowing the efficient filing of documents, the CM/ECF system provides practitioners and the public with the ability to monitor a case docket and receive timely notification of all documents filed. Once a practitioner is registered with the CM/ECF system and has filed a Notice of Appearance, the practitioner will automatically begin receiving docket notifications for that case.

Notice of Docket Activity. An electronic notification generated by the CM/ECF system will be transmitted by e-mail to all representatives in a case when a party or representative files a document with the Clerk's Office or when the court enters an order or takes other public actions in a case. (The Clerk's Office will also mail notices, orders, and pleadings to unrepresented parties.)

For ease of use, the docket-activity e-mail will usually contain a hyperlink back to the court's docket sheet or the document in question. This allows the practitioner to easily click on the link and view and/or print the activity or document docketed.

Viewing a Case Document. The CM/ECF system can also be used at any time to view a case's docket by going to the court's website and accessing the tab "Electronic Filing," then "Case Docket Reports," and finally the link for e-filing. You may then search the docket by party name, attorney name, or case number. When accessing the docket for a case, the user must click on the case number rather than the party names in the caption in order to view the General Docket Report. Recent docket activity will then be displayed. Click on "Full Docket" at the top of this screen and then "Run Docket Report" to see the full docket for the appeal. If a docket entry is preceded by a blue box, you may click on that box to see the document that was filed.

When accessing the docket for a case, the user must click on the "Case No." rather than the "Case" caption in order to view the General Docket Report.

---

b. Filing and Service (Rule 25)

Rule 25 governs when a paper is required or permitted to be filed in the court. Consult the rule for details on form of filing (mail, fax), timeliness requirements for paper filings, required service, manner of service, and proof of service.

PART 3

Starting the Process

I. Overview of the Appeal Process

The following is a brief overview of the appeal process:

- a Notice of Appeal is filed;
- VA files a Notice of Transmittal and the BVA decision;
- VA sends a copy of the Record Before the Agency (RBA) to counsel for the veteran;
- the veteran resolves any disputes over the RBA with counsel for the Secretary;
- the Clerk of Court issues a notice for the veteran to file a brief within 60 days;
- the Clerk of Court issues an order scheduling a Prebriefing Conference and requiring the veteran to file a Conference Memorandum at least 14 days in advance of the conference;[1]
- a Prebriefing Conference is held;
- briefs are filed—Veteran's Opening Brief, Secretary's Brief, and Veteran's Reply Brief;
- the Secretary (sometimes referred to as the VA counsel) files a Record of Proceedings (ROP) and serves all parties;
- the case is reviewed by the court's Central Legal Staff (CLS), which prepares a bench memo that includes a possible disposition;
- the case is assigned to a single judge;
- the judge decides whether a panel will be convened;
- oral argument may be ordered in cases assigned to a panel;

1. An unrepresented party is not required to file a Prebriefing Conference Memorandum.

- the case is decided;
- the parties may file a Motion for Reconsideration or review;
- a judgment is issued;
- any appeal to the United States Court of Appeals for the Federal Circuit (CAFC or Federal Circuit);
- mandate is issued; and
- if no appeal is filed, application for attorneys' fees under the Equal Access to Justice Act (EAJA).

Each of these events will be discussed in further detail.

II. Filing the Notice of Appeal

A. How to Appeal and Time for Appeal

1. FORM OF NOTICE OF APPEAL (RULE 3)

A person who is adversely affected by a Board decision may appeal to the court.[2] In order to appeal, a written Notice of Appeal must first be filed with the court. See figure on the next page.

a. Notice of Appeal.

The Notice of Appeal must include:

- the name, address, and phone number of the veteran and the VA claims file number;
- a reasonable identification of the Board's decision being appealed by including, e.g., the date of the Board's decision being appealed and the Board docket number; and
- a Notice of Appearance and fee or retainer agreement, if filed by a representative.

A suggested form for the Notice of Appeal can be found in the Appendix of the Rules of Practice and Procedure as well as on the

2. It is possible to have the Board reconsider its decision. A veteran may request a reconsideration in writing by identifying an error of fact or law. If reconsideration is requested within the original 120-day appeal period, then the appeal period is tolled. A new 120-day appeal period begins to run from the date of either the new Board decision, if reconsideration is granted, or notification that reconsideration has been denied. If the request is granted, then the original Board decision is nullified, and a new decision will be issued. If the request is denied, then the next step is an appeal to the CAVC.

court's website under "Court Forms." Using this exact form is not required, and while failure to include the required content listed above does not affect the validity of the appeal, it may delay the appeal and may be grounds for dismissal of the appeal.

Form: Notice of Appeal to the CAVC

UNITED STATES COURT OF APPEALS FOR VETERANS CLAIMS

NOTICE OF APPEAL

The following named appellant appeals to the Court from a final Board of Veterans' Appeals (BVA) decision. The Board's decision was dated ____________________.

______________________ Appellant's printed name	______________________ VA claims file number
______________________	______________________ Appellant's telephone number
______________________	
______________________ Appellant's address	______________________ Signature of person filing this notice

Only if this Notice of Appeal is filed by a representative, check one of the following:

☐ My Notice of Appearance is attached.

☐ My representation is limited to the filing of this Notice of Appeal, and I aver to the Court, in accordance with Rule 46(b)(2), that the appellant has been advised, or alternatively will be advised, of the appellant's responsibility to abide by the Court's Rules of Practice and Procedure, including the need to timely serve and submit for filing a brief. *(Complete items below).*

______________________ Representative's printed name	______________________ Representative's phone number
______________________	______________________ Representative's fax number
______________________	
______________________ Representative's address	______________________ Representative's email address

INSTRUCTIONS

Send this Notice of Appeal (NOA) (original only) to:

Clerk, US Court of Appeals for Veterans Claims
625 Indiana Avenue, NW, Suite 900
Washington, DC 20004-2950

The NOA will be timely if it is properly addressed to the Court and bears a legible postmark affixed by the United States Postal Service (USPS) within 120 days after the mailing date of the BVA decision that you are appealing. A postage-metered date imprint other than one affixed by USPS does not qualify.

You may send this NOA by facsimile transmission to (202) 501-5848 or by means other than US mail. If you do that, or if you mail the NOA and it does not bear a legible USPS postmark, the NOA will be late if it arrives at the Court after the 120-day time limit.

There is a $50 filing fee for an appeal. Send a check or money order, payable to "US Court of Appeals for Veterans Claims," with this NOA. Do not send cash. To request a waiver of the filing fee, attach a completed Form 4 (Declaration of Financial Hardship).

The Notice of Appeal is not required to comply with Rule 32. (This rule covers the format of briefs, appendices, and other documents and includes rules on typeface, spacing, binding, length, and so forth.) If, however, you create your own notice of appeal form, it is recommended that it follow Rule 32.

b. Filing the Notice of Appeal

The Notice of Appeal may be filed either by mail or fax. A current mailing address and fax number for the court can be found on the court's website or in Rule 3. The Notice of Appeal may also be submitted via e-mail to esubmission@uscourts.cavc.gov. The court will acknowledge a Notice of Appeal filed by e-mail with an autoreply that the e-mail was received.

You should contact the court to confirm receipt of a faxed Notice of Appeal as the court is not responsible for faxes that are not received.

---

2. FILING FEE

The $50.00 fee for filing the Notice of Appeal is nonrefundable. The fee may be paid by check or money order made payable to "U.S. Court of Appeals for Veterans Claims." If the filing fee is paid by check or money order, it should be promptly mailed to the court. It is a good practice to include a photocopy of the letter transmitting the check, the check, and a stamped return envelope with a request that the Clerk datestamp the check as received and return the copy for your file. You should note the CAVC docket number, if one has been assigned, on your check and refer to it in your letter.

If you fax or e-mail your Notice of Appeal, you must mail the filing fee so that the court receives it no later than 14 days after the fax or e-mail was sent.

---

3. WAIVER OF FILING FEE (RULE 24)

The court may waive payment of the $50.00 filing fee when a Declaration of Financial Hardship is filed. The form for the declaration can be found on the court's website under "Court Forms" and "Declaration of Financial Hardship" (see figure below). Only the veteran, not the representative, should sign this form. Alternatively, a practitioner may prepare his or her own declaration if it contains all of the same information called for in the court's form.

Form: Declaration of Financial Hardship

UNITED STATES COURT OF APPEALS FOR VETERANS CLAIMS

DECLARATION OF FINANCIAL HARDSHIP

Docket No. ________

______________________________, Appellant/Petitioner,

v.

Secretary of Veterans Affairs, Appellee/Respondent.

I am the appellant/petitioner. I declare by my signature below, that payment of the fifty dollar ($50.00) filing fee required by Rule 3(f) or Rule 21(a) of the Court's Rules of Practice and Procedure would be a financial hardship for me.

Pursuant to 28 U.S.C. § 1746, I certify, under penalty of perjury under the laws of the United States of America, that the foregoing is true and correct.

______________________________ ______________________

Signature of Appellant/Petitioner Date

(To be signed by Appellant, NOT Appellant's representative.)

****

INSTRUCTIONS

Send this Declaration (original only) to:

Clerk, U.S. Court of Appeals for Veterans Claims
625 Indiana Avenue, NW, Suite 900
Washington, DC 20004-2950

***OR** Fax (202) 501-5848*

If the veteran intends to file a Declaration of Financial Hardship, you should submit it along with the Notice of Appeal and your Notice of Appearance. Failure to promptly submit the filing fee or file the Declaration of Financial Hardship may prompt the court to issue an order to show cause why the appeal should not be dismissed. Such a show-cause order will generally allow a represented veteran seven days to comply.

The Declaration of Financial Hardship must be filed through the CM/ECF system if the veteran is represented. A scanned version may be filed electronically (the requirement for using a PDF converter does not apply to this form). The form must be signed, and a declaration lacking a signature will be returned. Self-represented veterans may also file a Declaration of Financial Hardship with a Notice of Appeal by submitting those forms to esubmission@uscourts.cavc.gov.

YIELD

If you fax your Notice of Appeal, you must mail or fax the Declaration of Financial Hardship so that the court receives it no later than 14 days after the fax was sent.

---

4. TIMING OF FILING NOTICE OF APPEAL (RULE 4)

The most crucial aspect of filing a Notice of Appeal is to file it within the proper time frame. The time for filing a Notice of Appeal cannot generally be extended. If a timely appeal is not received, the Board decision becomes final.

a. Notice of Appeal Due Date

Rule 4 explains the time for appealing and states that the Notice of Appeal must be received by the Clerk no later than 120 days after the date on which the Board mailed the notice of the decision. That date is the date mailed to the last known address of the veteran and the veteran's representative. This is presumed to be the date stamped on the front of the Board's decision, unless a later date is shown by, for example, the date of the Board's letter transmitting the decision to the veteran. This is why it is important for veterans and their representatives to keep their address information with the Board current.

Date Stamped on Board Decision + 120 Days = Date Notice of Appeal Is Due. 120 Days, *Not* Four Months.

When the Notice of Appeal Is Received by the Court. A Notice of Appeal is considered "received" under the following circumstances:

- date of legible United States Postal Service (USPS) postmark (postage-metered date imprint does not qualify); Rule 4(a)(1) or
- date of actual receipt by the Clerk when the Notice of Appeal is sent via fax, e-mail, or a service other than USPS.

Because the date is so crucial to a Notice of Appeal, you should keep evidence of the date on which you sent the notice to the court. If the Notice of Appeal is sent by e-mail, it is a good practice to send a blind carbon copy to yourself, as this copy will include the date of transmission.

You may send a Notice of Appeal via a service other than the USPS (e.g., FedEx or UPS); however, without a legible USPS postmark, the Notice of Appeal will only be timely if it is *actually received* in the Clerk's office within the 120-day appeal period.

5. NOTICE OF APPEARANCE (RULE 46(b))

a. When to File a Notice of Appearance

No practitioner may act as a representative for a veteran or other appellant without first filing a Notice of Appearance.

If the person filing the appeal is represented at the time of filing the Notice of Appeal, the Notice of Appearance must accompany the Notice of Appeal (Rule 3). When filing a Notice of Appearance with a Notice of Appeal, neither form is filed with the CM/ECF system. Filing with the CM/ECF system requires a court docket number. At the time the Notice of Appeal is filed, no docket number exists.

A law firm cannot enter an "appearance." A Notice of Appearance must be filed under the name of a person admitted to the bar of the court. Rule 46(b)(1)(E).

b. Limited Appearance—Only for the Purposes of Filing the Appeal

A Notice of Appearance is not required if a practitioner files only a Notice of Appeal for a veteran and specifies that the appearance by the practitioner is limited to the filing of the Notice of Appeal. This is referred to as a "Limited Appearance Notice of Appeal." Rule 46(b)(2). In that case, the Notice of Appeal must also include the name, address, and telephone number of the practitioner. In addition, the practitioner filing the Limited Appearance Notice of Appeal must aver that "the Veteran has been advised, or, alternatively, will be advised, of the Veteran's responsibility to abide by the Court's Rules of Practice and Procedure, including the need to timely serve and submit for filing a brief." Rule 46(b)(2)(A)(ii). If the practitioner avers that the veteran has not been, but will be, so informed, the court will treat the practitioner as counsel of record until the practitioner informs the court that the veteran has been duly informed.

c. A Copy of Your Fee Agreement

You must file a copy of your fee or retainer agreement with the veteran (or similar document explaining the fee arrangement) with the court. A copy of the fee agreement with the client is required even if the representation is pro bono. Rule 46(b)(1)(A). The fee or retainer agreement must be attached as a separate document to your e-mail submitting the Notice of Appeal or separately filed using the CM/ECF system if you enter a Notice of Appearance after the appeal is docketed.

d. Form for Notice of Appearance

A Notice of Appearance (see figure on the next page) can be found in the Appendix to the Court's Rules of Practice and Procedure or downloaded from the court's website under "Court Forms."

Form: Notice of Appearance

UNITED STATES COURT OF APPEALS FOR VETERANS CLAIMS

NOTICE OF APPEARANCE

______________________________, ◯ Appellant,
◯ Petitioner,

v. Docket No. ____________

Secretary of Veterans Affairs, Appellee / Respondent.

1. Please enter my appearance for ◯ the appellant or petitioner
◯ the Secretary
◯ the Intervenor
◯ Amicus Curiae: ______________________________.

2. I am:
◯ admitted to practice before this Court as: ◯ attorney ◯ non-attorney practitioner
◯ awaiting admission to practice; my application was submitted on (date)__________
◯ seeking to appear in this case only, under Rule 46(b)(1)(F); my motion is attached.

3. I am:
◯ the lead representative of record. I will accept service for the party and will inform all of the party's co-representatives of matters served upon me.
◯ not the lead representative of record, but am joining as co-representative.
◯ replacing the lead representative of record, who has:
◯ has been permitted or is seeking to withdraw
◯ remains as co-representative

4. If I am representing the appellant, petitioner, or intervenor, my representation is:
◯ pursuant to the attached fee agreement. If the fee agreement provides for direct payment out of past-due benefits under 38 U.S.C. § 5904, a copy has been served on counsel for the Secretary. If the fee agreement provides for a contingent fee, it also provides for an offset of any fees awarded under the Equal Access to Justice Act (EAJA), 28 U.S.C. § 2412(d).
◯ without charge to the appellant, petitioner, or intervenor; however it is subject to the attached retainer agreement.
◯ pursuant to the fee/retainer agreement already on record in this case.

/s/ ______________________________ ______________________________
Signature Date

______________________________ ______________________________
Printed name Veterans Service Org. if R. 46(a)(2)(B) applies.

____

______________________________ ______________________________

______________________________ Signature and printed name and address of
Address supervising attorney, if R. 46(a)(2)(A) applies.

______________________________ ______________________________

Telephone number Email address

Attachments: ☐ Application and motion to appear under Rule 46(b)(1)(F)
☐ Fee agreement ☐ Retainer agreement

If you lose touch with your client at any point during the appeal process, you should make every reasonable attempt to contact your client, including a phone call, e-mail, and letter via U.S. mail. If these efforts fail, then you should nonetheless continue to represent your client using your best judgment.

Alternatively, a practitioner may file his or her own Notice of Appearance form if it contains all the details called for in the court's form. But the court strongly recommends and prefers that you use its form.

e. How to File a Notice of Appearance

A Notice of Appearance, fee agreement, or Declaration of Financial Hardship (see previous section), submitted concurrently with a Notice of Appeal, may be attached as separate PDF documents to a single e-mail and sent to esubmission@uscourts.cavc.gov. The court will acknowledge the submissions by return e-mail. It is a good idea to send a blind carbon copy of your e-mail to yourself so that you will have a record of what was submitted and when.

For an existing appeal, use the CM/ECF system to file your Notice of Appearance and fee or retainer agreement. Instructions can be found in the court's e-filing training modules.

One frequent mistake when e-filing a Notice of Appearance is the failure to select the "Add Attorney" button after finding the attorney's name.

B. After the Notice of Appeal Is Filed

After receiving the Notice of Appeal, the Clerk will docket the appeal and send a Notice of Docketing to all parties notifying them of the date the appeal was received. The Secretary has 30 days from the date of docketing to file a copy of the Board's decision with the Clerk. A copy of the Board's decision will also be served on the veteran at this time. The copy will show the date the Board's decision was mailed (the date from which the 120-day time period for filing the Notice of Appeal is calculated), the filing date of any motion for its reconsideration or vacatur, and the date and nature of any action on such a motion.

You should carefully compare the Board's decision filed by the VA with the decision the practitioner intends to appeal to ensure they are the same. If the decisions are not the same, contact counsel for the Secretary to see whether they are willing to file an amended copy. If the Secretary is not willing to correct the error, then you will need to file an objection with the court.

C. Expedited Proceedings (Rule 47)

If your client is elderly or in particularly ill health, you may consider asking the court for expedited proceedings to help ensure that your client will enjoy VA benefits during his or her lifetime.

1. MOTION FOR EXPEDITED PROCEEDINGS

On a party's motion for good cause shown, on written agreement of the parties, or on its own initiative, the court may order that any matter before the court be expedited for some or all procedural steps.

Any of the following reasons may constitute good cause:

1. a serious health condition that makes the death of the veteran[3] imminent, as shown by a physician's statement (including identification of the physician's licensing authority and current license number);
2. the advanced age (over 75 years) of the veteran and a state of failing health due to a nontemporary condition, as shown by a physician's statement (including identification of the physician's licensing authority and current license number), such

---

3. This pertains as well to some other petitioner, such as the veteran's spouse, if the veteran has already died.

that expeditious proceedings are necessary to avoid an injustice to the veteran; or

3. any other exceptional circumstances that make expeditious proceedings necessary to avoid an injustice to the veteran, as shown by credible evidence.

Consideration of good cause under clauses (2) and (3) of this subsection may take into account the overall caseload of a judge or judges.

2. FILING AND SERVICE OF PAPERS

Expedited proceedings will be scheduled as directed by the court. Unless otherwise ordered, the veteran's principal brief must be served and filed no later than 20 days after the RBA has been served on the veteran; the Secretary's Brief must be served and filed no later than 20 days after service of the veteran's opening brief; and any reply brief must be served and filed no later than 10 days after service of the Secretary's Brief. Unless otherwise ordered, the time to file the ROP under Rule 28.1(b)(3) is seven days. *See* Part 5, § IV, *infra*.

3. FORM AND LENGTH OF BRIEFS

Briefs filed under this rule must comply with Rules 28 and 32, except that principal briefs must be limited to 15 pages, reply briefs must be limited to 7 pages, and a Table of Authorities is not required.

YIELD

Be sure that motions to expedite contain the doctor's licensing authority and current license number. Rule 47(a)(1).

PART 4

Prebriefing Process

I. Record Before the Agency

After a Notice of Appeal is filed and docketed, VA counsel creates the Record Before the Agency (RBA) and serves it on the veteran's counsel.

A. Designation of Record Before the Agency (Rule 10)

1. FORM AND CONTENT OF THE RECORD

The RBA will contain documents from the veteran's claims file and other material that counsel for the Secretary believes are potentially relevant to the appeal. The RBA should include all relevant materials that were in the veteran's claims file "on the date the Board issued the decision from which the appeal was taken." Rule 10(a). Note that documents postdating the Board's decision on appeal will generally not be included in the RBA and may not be considered by the court.

The RBA generally includes:

- all military service medical records;
- all VA medical records;
- any private medical treatment records the veteran has submitted or requested that the VA procure; and

- all decisions by the VA Regional Office and Board pertaining to the claim at issue and any other claim the veteran pursued in the past.[1]

The RBA will generally come on a CD-ROM in searchable PDF format. The first document in the RBA will be the Board's decision, and materials will generally appear in reverse chronological order (most recent documents first).

2. HOW DO I GET THE RBA?

The Secretary should send the RBA no later than 60 days after the date of the Notice of Docketing. If you have entered an appearance on behalf of a veteran, the Secretary will send the RBA to you. In some instances, the Secretary may request an extension of time to serve the RBA. It is always advisable to be agreeable and consent to such a request, as this builds goodwill for the future.

3. WHAT SHOULD I DO ONCE I RECEIVE THE RBA?

Once the RBA arrives, you should review the record to determine whether there are any missing pages. Also, you should cross-check the Board's decision and make sure the evidence it cites appears on the CD-ROM.

In addition, to ensure accuracy of the information on the CD-ROM, you may compare the data on it with the documents in the client's original VA file, referred to as a "claims file."

The method of comparing the RBA to the veteran's claims file depends on whether the file is maintained as a "paper file" or a "virtual file." Some claims files may be a combination of paper and virtual files.

---

1. According to Rule 10(a), the RBA must include "a list of any record matter that cannot be duplicated." Presumably, this list might include X-rays or other such material that could not be included in the RBA.

a. Reviewing Paper Claims Files

If the veteran has a paper claims file, there are two ways to compare the RBA to the veteran's claims file, depending on whether you are located in Washington, D.C., or elsewhere. The VA will temporarily transfer a paper file to the VA General Counsel's Office in Washington during the pendency of the appeal.

i. Reviewing Paper and Virtual Claims Files in Washington, D.C.

The VA General Counsel Professional Staff Group VII represents the Secretary in all appeals to the CAVC. In January 2013, the VA General Counsel and the Veterans Benefits Administration established new procedures governing an attorney's access to the original VA claims file. In Washington, D.C., claims files may now be reviewed only at the VA facility located at 1722 I Street, N.W., and only on Tuesdays, Wednesdays, and Thursdays between 8:00 am and 4:00 pm. Reviews are by appointment only.

An attorney wishing to review a claims file must contact the VA General Counsel attorney representing the Secretary and propose a date and time for the review. These requests must be made at least seven days in advance of the proposed date for the review. Advance notice allows time for the VA attorney to arrange to have the claims file moved from the General Counsel's Office to the I Street location. On the date of the review, the reviewer must present valid photo identification to be admitted to the VA offices.

You must provide the VA personnel with a copy of a written consent form, executed by the veteran, granting VA permission to allow you to review the veteran's VA files, both paper and electronic. Electronic files are referred to as virtual or "VVA" files. The VA will mail this consent form to you, or the client, shortly after the Notice of Appeal is filed.

In addition, you will be asked to complete a form certifying that you have not added anything to or deleted anything from the file and further certifying that you have provided the VA with a copy of the executed consent form. You must provide your own laptop if you

Form: Consent to Release of Information from VA Files

CONSENT TO RELEASE OF INFORMATION FROM VA FILES

By signing this form, I hereby request and authorize the Secretary of Veterans Affairs to release to the U.S. Court of Appeals for Veterans Claims documents and other material from VA files that are relevant to the instant litigation, including any decision rendered by the Board of Veterans' Appeals relevant to this litigation.

In the event information to be released includes information regarding drug abuse, infection with human immunodeficiency virus (HIV), alcoholism or alcohol abuse, or sickle cell anemia protected by 38 U.S.C. § 7332, I specifically consent to that disclosure as well.

I understand that any documents and materials that might otherwise be protected by 38 U.S.C. 5701, and any Board of Veterans' Appeals decision will become public unless I seek and am granted a sealing of the record by the Court pursuant to the Court's E-Rule 8 and Rules of Practice and Procedure 48 of the Court. Redisclosure of my medical records by those receiving the above-authorized information may be accomplished without any further written authorization and may no longer be protected.

I may revoke this consent to disclosure at any time, but if not revoked before action is taken in reliance upon it, this consent shall automatically expire on the date this litigation is withdrawn; or, if not withdrawn, on the date of final decision by the U.S. Court of Appeals for Veterans Claims, or final resolution of any subsequent appeals to the U.S. Court of Appeals for the Federal Circuit or the Supreme Court of the United Sates, whichever comes last.

______________________________ ________________

Name (Please Print) Docket Number

______________________________ ________________

Signature (Indicate if Court-Appointed Guardian) Date

Please see back of form for instructions

Revised 12/23/2009

INSTRUCTIONS

This form must be personally signed by the veteran or beneficiary to whom the records pertain, or his/her legal guardian. Legal counsel or representative should not sign it.

In the case of a deceased veteran, the next of kin, executor, administrator or other personal representative of the decedent's estate must sign the form. In cases in which the litigant is not the veteran, beneficiary or personal representative of the decedent's estate, the litigant must make arrangements to obtain the veteran's, beneficiary's or representative's signature, or move the Court for a specific order for release of documents and material in the custody of the Department of Veterans Affairs.

Failure to properly consent to the release of documents and material in the custody of the Department of Veterans Affairs may result in a delay in the pending litigation.

intend to compare the paper claims file to the RBA on the CD-ROM served by the VA. The General Counsel will permit you to make a reasonable number of photocopies without charge.

Items Required to Review Claims Files at VA General Counsel's Office in Washington, D.C.

- Personal identification.
- A copy of the signed consent form from the veteran.
- A laptop computer and CD-ROM or a paper copy of the veteran's RBA printed from the CD-ROM.

b. Reviewing Paper Claims Files Outside the Washington, D.C., Area

If you are located outside the Washington metropolitan area, you may ask the VA in writing to provide a paper copy of the veteran's file. The VA generally takes approximately 60 days or more from the request date to provide a hard copy.

If you are located outside the Washington area, you should request the copy of the client's claims file as early as possible after filing the Notice of Appeal. The VA may take two months or more to respond to the request. In the alternative, the practitioner can try to make arrangements with other local Washington practitioners to conduct the review.

c. Reviewing Virtual Files

The VA is in the process of transitioning from paper files to virtual (i.e., electronic) files. Thus, the RBAs in some cases may consist of a paper file only, while some cases may consist of a partial paper file and a partial virtual file. All VA claims files will eventually be electronic. Paper files are maintained at the VA General Counsel's Office while a court appeal is pending, and virtual files are maintained by the VA Compensation & Pension Service.

You can review virtual files at the nearest VA Regional Office. In order to review virtual files, you must contact the Fee Coordinator at the Regional Office and request an appointment to review the files. A list of the Regional Offices can be found at http://www2.va.gov/guide/home.asp. This webpage lists Regional offices, as well as healthcare facilities and cemeteries.

Time Limit for Reviewing the File

The CAVC Rules allow 14 days for a veteran to respond to the RBA. Rule 10(b). This time is extended by five days because the VA serves the RBA by mail. Rule 26(c)(1). These 19 days run from the date of the Certificate of Service transmitting a copy of the RBA.

If you need more time, you must contact the VA General Counsel and request consent to a Motion for Extension of Time to Review the RBA. *See* Rule 26(b). After you file the motion, the CAVC will generally issue an order granting an unopposed Motion for Extension of Time within 24 to 48 hours.

4. Pages Missing from the RBA

If you (or the reviewer) determine that pages in the claims file are missing from the RBA, then the VA General Counsel Group VII file room personnel will permit the person reviewing the file to copy the missing documents.

Next, you should determine whether the pages missing from the RBA are relevant to the issues on appeal and, if so, contact counsel for the VA. The e-mail address for the VA counsel assigned to the appeal can be found on the court's docketing notices for each case, and their phone number appears at the top of the court's docket sheet. VA counsel may be able to correct the error without the need to file a motion.

5. Disputing the RBA

Keep in mind that you have only 19 days after service of the RBA to dispute the record by motion. Therefore, if the issue is not resolved with VA counsel, you must file a motion responding to correct the RBA. Under Rule 10(b), the motion must describe the good-faith efforts the parties have made to resolve the dispute. Therefore, contacting VA counsel is an important step in order to show you made a good-faith effort.

YIELD

Checking the accuracy of the RBA is an important step that should not be overlooked. If a relevant page is missing, the court cannot evaluate the missing evidence, which may prove critical to your case.

If no pages are missing, then it is time to begin analyzing the merits of the case.

SAMPLE: Veteran's Response Disputing the Record Before the Agency

IN THE UNITED STATES COURT OF APPEALS
FOR VETERANS CLAIMS

[VETERAN'S NAME],	)	
	)	
Appellant,	)	
	)	
v.	)	[CAVC APPEAL NO.]
	)	
[NAME OF CURRENT SECRETARY],	)	
Secretary of Veterans Affairs,	)	
	)	
Appellee.	)	

APPELLANT'S RESPONSE DISPUTING
THE RECORD BEFORE THE AGENCY

Pursuant to U.S. Vet. App. Rule 10(b), [VETERAN'S NAME], Appellant, hereby moves the Court for an order directing Appellee to include records that were omitted from the Record Before the Agency. The Record Before the Agency served by Appellee fails to include a number of documents from the administrative record before the Board of Veterans' Appeals in the captioned appeal. The missing records are:

[INSERT MISSING RECORDS]

The undersigned contacted counsel for Appellee, but was unable to resolve the dispute.

Respectfully submitted,

/s/ [E-SIGNATURE]
[ATTORNEY NAME]
[FIRM ADDRESS]
[PHONE NO.]

Attorney for Appellant

6. The Difference Between the "Record Before the Agency" and the "Record of Proceedings"

The RBA, as explained above, is a copy of materials contained in the claims file and other material from the record before the Board relevant to the Board's decision on appeal. Therefore, as the RBA contains the entirety of the veteran's claims file, not all of the RBA will be relevant to the appeal. The RBA is not filed with the court.

In contrast, the Record of Proceedings (ROP) contains only the Board's decision along with any document from the RBA cited in any brief or any other documents relevant to the appeal. After the briefing is complete, the Secretary prepares and files the ROP with the court. *See* Rule 28.1. *See* the "Recording of Proceedings" section for further information about the ROP.

II. Staff (Prebriefing) Conference with the Court (Rule 33)

The Staff Conference, also known as the Prebriefing Conference, is conducted by phone between a veteran's counsel and VA counsel for the appeal. A member of the court's Central Legal Staff (CLS) conducts this conference. The conference, usually conducted by phone, is intended to narrow or resolve the issues on appeal before briefing.

The court strongly encourages the parties to discuss settlement or alternative disposition of the matters on appeal. As part of the conference proceedings, the court requires that the veteran prepare a Prebriefing Conference Memorandum.

The Prebriefing Conference and Conference Memorandum are a good way to resolve the dispute before the briefing process, so it is important to do a thorough job. If the Prebriefing Conference does not result in an agreement to dispose of the appeal, the Conference Memorandum will provide a valuable guide for the veteran's Opening Brief.

A. Timing

The court will schedule a conference to occur approximately 30 days before the due date for the veteran's Opening Brief. The court schedules the conference after it sends the Notice to File Brief. The order for a conference will require a memorandum to be served by e-mail on VA counsel and the CLS, but not filed with the court, 14 days in advance of the conference.

Rescheduling the Conference. Under Rule 33, it is possible to reschedule the conference upon a showing of good cause. If you need to reschedule, contact VA counsel and then the CLS attorney who will conduct the conference as soon as possible to coordinate either a new time, date, or both.

B. Settlement Authority

Before the conference, contact the veteran to explain the possible outcomes of the conference and obtain authority to settle the case or enter into a joint remand agreement with VA counsel.

As can be seen from the sample order, the court typically orders that the representatives of both parties have the authority to enter into a joint resolution or settlement to the extent authorized by the client, or be within immediate contact with the veteran during the conference.

SAMPLE ORDER: Order for a Staff Conference

Not published

UNITED STATES COURT OF APPEALS FOR VETERANS CLAIMS

No [redacted]

[redacted] APPELLANT,

V.

ERIC K. SHINSEKI,
SECRETARY OF VETERANS AFFAIRS, APPELLEE.

ORDER

The appellant, who is represented, appeals a December 23, 2011, Board of Veterans' Appeals decision. A "Notice to File Brief" within 60 days was mailed to the appellant on June 13, 2012. Accordingly, it is

ORDERED that the Court will initiate a telephonic briefing conference on July 27, 2012, at 1:30 PM (ET). It will be conducted by Elizabeth Hessman-Talbot, Esq., of the Court's Central Legal Staff (CLS), and this conference may be rescheduled by the Court only upon a showing of good cause. It is further

ORDERED that not later than 14 days prior to the scheduled conference, the appellant's counsel or representative shall submit to the Secretary and the Central Legal Staff (by e-mail or fax), a summary of the issues that the appellant intends to raise in the appeal before the Court, to include citations to the relevant authorities and the pertinent documents in the record. The appellant's counsel or representative shall also file **with the Clerk** and serve on the Secretary a **separate** certificate of service that includes the date of the appellant's submission to the Secretary and the Central Legal Staff, the specific manner of the service (e-mail or fax) and the names and addresses of the persons served. E-mail submissions shall be sent to the Central Legal Staff at **CLS-Calendar@uscourts.cavc.gov**. Fax submissions shall be sent to CLS fax number at **(202)585-3951.** It is further

ORDERED that the attorney or representative for both parties shall attend the conference with the authority to enter into a joint resolution of the appeal or settlement to the extent authorized by the client or be within immediate contact with such a person during the staff conference. The parties shall jointly notify the Court if the parties reach agreement on the disposition of any or all issues prior to the conference.

DATED [redacted]

FOR THE COURT:

GREGORY O. BLOCK
Clerk of the Court

By: /s/ [redacted]
Deputy Clerk

Absent an order of the court, the time period for taking any action under the court's rules, including preparation of the veteran's Opening Brief, is not tolled for the time required to prepare for the staff conference.

C. The Prebriefing Conference Memorandum

The Prebriefing Conference Memorandum summarizes the issues you intend to raise in the appeal, including citations to relevant authorities and pertinent RBA documents. The memorandum is due 14 days before the staff conference. The purpose of the memorandum is to facilitate resolution of the case without the need for full briefing. Accordingly, this requires a practitioner to set forth concisely and persuasively the factual and legal issues on appeal, the veteran's positions, and the factual and legal authority supporting the veteran's positions so that the VA can see the strength of the case.

The positions in the prebriefing memorandum and during the conference are not binding; therefore, if the case proceeds to briefing, arguments advanced at the conference need not be included in the brief, and different arguments may be made in the brief.

1. FORMAT OF MEMORANDUM

The memorandum must comply with Rules 32 and 33 and must adhere to the following:

- the memorandum must be limited to *ten pages* (not including submission of exhibits or material from the RBA);
- the memorandum must use letter-sized pages (8.5 x 11 inches) with at least one-inch-wide margins from all edges;
- the text must be limited to 13-point or larger-sized typeface (*see* Rule 32 for more information on monospaced typeface);
- the text must be double spaced;
- quotations of 50 words or more must be single spaced;

- footnotes must be single spaced and meet the same typeface requirements as the rest of the memorandum;
- pages must be numbered in the center of the bottom margin; and
- the signature, printed name, address, and telephone number of the representative must appear on the document.

A sample Prebriefing Conference Memorandum appears in the Appendices.

2. SERVING THE MEMORANDUM

The Prebriefing Conference Memorandum may be submitted either by e-mail or fax to the CLS. Current contact information appears in Rule 33, but as of this printing, the e-mail address for submissions is CLS-Calendar@uscourts.cavc.gov, and the fax number is (202) 585-3951. The memorandum should also be e-mailed to VA counsel for the appeal. The e-mail address for the VA counsel assigned to the appeal can be found on the court's docketing notices for each case.

In addition to submitting the memorandum by e-mail or fax, you must file a Certificate of Service with the court that includes the date of the submission of the memorandum, the manner of service (e-mail or fax), and the names and addresses of the persons served. You should file this Certificate of Service using the CM/ECF system.

STOP The memorandum must be submitted by e-mail to the CLS and may not be filed with the court. Only the Certificate of Service must be filed with the court.

D. The Conference

The conference is held between the counsel for the veteran and counsel for the VA and is conducted by a CAVC staff attorney from the CLS. The conference occurs by phone, or in rare instances, the date and time specified in the conference order. As with the Prebriefing Conference Memorandum, statements made during the conference cannot be disclosed to the judge unless the parties agree in writing to that disclosure.

The CLS staff members have been provided additional mediation training in order to help the conference move smoothly toward a resolution. Typically, as the counsel for the veteran has already submitted the veteran's positions in the Prebriefing Conference Memorandum, the CLS attorney will begin the conference by asking the VA attorney for his or her response. The conference may proceed in many different ways—VA counsel may ask for clarification of arguments, he or she may disagree with the positions in the Prebriefing Conference Memorandum, or he or she may agree and suggest a remand appeal or outright settlement of the case.

In case the VA attorney disagrees with the positions advanced in the Prebriefing Conference Memorandum, it is helpful for you to draft key questions regarding the appeal's strongest points before the conference (e.g., "Could you explain how the Board properly addressed the standard under X case?" "Could you please explain why you don't think the precedent in Y is applicable here?").

But keep in mind, counsel for the VA will have only that authority granted by their supervisor to resolve the appeal by remand or settlement. They may, however, be willing to ask the supervisor to reconsider a remand or settlement if you present a persuasive argument.

III. Settlements and Remands

A. How Is a Joint Motion for Remand Different from a Settlement?

A Joint Motion for Remand and a settlement are usually treated differently. A Joint Motion for Remand is filed with the court and, when granted, terminates the CAVC appeal. The order granting the joint motion constitutes the judgment and mandate of the court. On the other hand, in the case of a settlement, the parties usually file a Joint Motion to Terminate the Appeal and attach the settlement agreement to that motion.

The administrative proceedings that follow a remand and a settlement also differ. The order granting a Joint Motion for Remand sends the appeal back to the Board. In a settlement, however, the VA typically agrees that the case will go from the VA Office of General Counsel directly to the Regional Office for implementation.

B. Settlement

1. WHAT DOES "SETTLEMENT" MEAN IN THIS CONTEXT?

Settlement in a veteran's appeal means that the case or claim is decided in the veteran's favor. Do not overlook the possibility of agreeing to settle some of a veteran's claims while agreeing to dismiss the remaining claims in exchange—especially in instances where this is the last opportunity for the veteran to prevail on the claim to be settled (such as a claim for service connection for a disability) absent new and material evidence. The veteran will have later opportunities to pursue the dropped claims (such as for increased disability ratings for an already service-connected disability).

2. ADVOCATING FOR A SETTLEMENT

When to Settle. You should advocate for a settlement early and often. To advocate for a settlement, contact VA counsel and clearly set forth the legal errors made by the Board. You may start advocating for a settlement even before the record is served.

The best candidates for settlement are cases in which the Board has made legal errors—in other words, in cases where the facts are not disputed, but the Board failed to apply correctly the law.

Consent from the Veteran. Of course, it is paramount that all settlements are negotiated and agreed to with the veteran's full understanding and consent. A settlement agreement can include an instruction for further proceedings by the Regional Office. If a case for service connection is settled, the settlement may also instruct the Regional Office to determine the disability rating for what is now a service-connected disability.

3. SETTLEMENT AGREEMENTS

Written Settlement Agreements. The VA will frequently not want to settle, preferring full briefing or a remand to a settlement. Therefore, it is important to get all settlement agreements in writing. If VA counsel agrees to settlement, then it may be best to allow VA counsel to prepare the first draft. The final agreement may involve some negotiations or revisions back and forth with VA counsel. The settlement agreement must be signed by counsel for both parties.

Joint Motion for Stay of Proceedings. After the parties reach agreement in principle on the terms for a settlement or Joint Motion for Remand, they typically file a Joint Motion for a Stay of Proceedings. Rule 5. This rule allows the Clerk to grant a motion to stay proceedings for up to 60 days. Rule 45(g)(5). Filing a motion does not stay proceedings. Only a court order granting the motion puts the stay into effect. While a Joint Motion for a Stay of Proceedings may be appropriate at any point during the appellate process, settlements and Joint Motions for Remand most typically occur before the veteran's Opening Brief is filed. The veteran may elect to file a motion for an extension of time as an alternative to a Joint Motion for a Stay of Proceedings to provide additional time to complete drafting the settlement or remand documents.

4. VOLUNTARY TERMINATION OR DISMISSAL (RULE 42)

Once the parties have executed a written settlement agreement, they must request that the court either terminate or dismiss the appeal.

Voluntary Termination. If the parties submit a Motion to Terminate an appeal based on a settlement agreement negotiated to take effect upon termination of the case by the court, then, under Rule 42, the Clerk may enter the case terminated.

Dismissal. The Clerk of Court can dismiss a matter on terms requested by a veteran, terms agreed upon by the parties, or terms previously fixed by the court if the veteran files a motion for dismissal. An appeal, petition, or application for attorneys' fees and expenses can be the subject of a Motion to Dismiss.

C. Joint Motions for Remand

A Joint Motion for Remand asks the court to vacate the Board's decision, either in whole or in part, and send the appeal back to the Board for further proceedings. It must be signed by attorneys for both parties. The joint motion usually acknowledges one or more mistakes by the Board in reaching its decision. These mistakes may include failure to consider a statute or regulation, failure to account for evidence favorable to the claimant, clearly erroneous findings of fact, basing the decision on an inadequate VA medical examination, inadequate reasons or bases for the Board's decision, or failure to consider issues reasonably raised by the RBA.

The joint motion must specifically state the reason for the remand and must also clearly state what, if any, parts of the Board's decision are not vacated. If, for example, the Board granted an increased disability rating for one disability, denied service connection for a second disability, and the client is satisfied with the increased rating, then the joint motion should specifically state that the increased rating should not be disturbed. The joint motion should give the Board specific guidance on what must be done on remand.

Either party may write the first draft of a Joint Motion for Remand. The other party will have an opportunity to review the draft and propose changes.

Include a reasonable amount of detail in the motion. For example, if the Board did not consider evidence favorable to the claimant, then state what that evidence is and where it can be found in the RBA. If the Board overlooked a favorable provision of a statute or regulation, it should be cited in the motion. A sample Joint Motion for Remand appears in the Appendices.

When the court grants the motion, the veteran will have an enforceable right to have the Board comply with the terms in the Joint Motion for Remand. Failure to comply can be enforced in a later appeal. Thus, it is important that the motion submitted to the court address all prejudicial errors in the Board decision being appealed.

D. Application for Attorneys' Fees Following Settlement or Remand

Even if the veteran agrees to terminate the appeal based on a settlement agreement or agrees to a Joint Motion for Remand, the veteran may still apply for attorneys' fees under the Equal Access to Justice Act (EAJA). The order granting either motion triggers the 30-day period during which the veteran's application for an award of attorneys' fees and expenses under the EAJA, 28 U.S.C. § 2412, will be timely. *See* the EAJA section for more information.

IV. Motions (Rule 27)

During the appeal, you may need to file various motions. These include, for example, a Joint Motion for Remand, Motion to Withdraw, Motion for Extension of Time, Motion to Stay Proceedings, Motion to Expedite Proceedings, Motion Disputing the RBA or ROP, and Motion to Amend (or Correct) a Pleading. Some additional tips related to specific motions can be found later in this section.

A. Content and Timing

Rule 27 sets forth requirements for the content of a motion. It must:

1. contain or be accompanied by any material required by any of the rules governing such a motion;
2. state with particularity the specific grounds on which it is based;
3. describe the relief sought;
4. ***not*** be accompanied by a proposed implementing order; and
5. a statement in compliance with Rule 27(a)(5); if the appellant is represented, indicate whether the motion is opposed and, if so, whether the moving party has been advised that a response in opposition will be filed.

YIELD

Any party may file a response or an opposition to a motion within 14 days after the motion is filed, except that any opposition to a motion for extension of time must be filed within five days. Rule 26(b)(2). The court may shorten or extend the time for responding to any motion.

If a party indicates that it is opposed to a motion but fails to file a written opposition, the court will treat the motion as unopposed. Rule 27(b)(2).

Regarding motions for procedural orders, the court may act at any time without awaiting a response. Any party who may be adversely affected by the action may, by motion, request that the court reconsider, vacate, or modify the action no later than ten days after the action is announced.

B. Format

Motions or responses must not exceed ten pages. As with all other court filings, it is important to either not include personal information or redact all personal information from the motion. *See* Rule 6. The formatting requirements in Rule 32 also apply to motions and responses, including:

- text must appear on letter-size pages (8.5 x 11 inches) with at least one-inch-wide margins from all edges;
- text must appear in 13-point or larger-sized typeface (*see* Rule 32 for more information on monospaced typeface);
- text must be double spaced;
- quotations of 50 words or more must be single spaced;
- footnotes must be single spaced and satisfy the same typeface requirements as the rest of the motion or response;
- pages must be numbered in the center of the bottom margin; and
- the e-signature, printed name, address, and telephone number of the representative must appear on the document.

C. Extensions of Time (Rule 26)

If needed, extensions up to a total of 45 days, based on a showing of good cause, are available for any particular filing. Extensions beyond a total of 45 days for a particular filing are granted only for extraordinary circumstances.

STOP The court may not extend the time for filing a Notice of Appeal or an application for attorneys' fees and expenses.

In addition to the content and format requirements of Rule 27, explained above, motions for extensions of time must also include:

- the original due date to be extended;
- the revised date sought;
- the total number of days of extension previously granted to the movant;
- the total number of days of extension previously granted to the other party(ies) in the case; and
- a statement in compliance with Rule 27(a)(5): If the appellant is represented, indicate whether the motion is opposed and, if so, whether the moving party has been advised that a response in opposition will be filed.

In some cases, when asked whether it opposes a motion, a party may respond that it "takes no position" on the motion. In such a case, the movant has *not* been informed that "the motion is opposed" or whether "a response in opposition will be filed."

With the exception of a motion for leave to file an out-of-time motion to extend time, a motion to extend time may *not* be combined with any other motion. Rule 26(d). The Clerk of Court will return any motion that violates this subsection.

YIELD A motion to extend time does not extend the date on which a pleading or other document is due to be filed with the court *unless* the court grants that motion.

Opposition to Motion for Extension of Time. Any opposition to a motion to extend time must be filed with the Clerk no later than five days after the motion to extend is filed. If no opposition is filed within five days, the court will treat the motion as unopposed. The Clerk may act on motions to extend time for good cause (but not for extraordinary circumstances) if the motion is consented to or not opposed within five days after service on the other party. *See* Rule 45(g)(4).

SAMPLE: Veteran's Unopposed Motion for Extension of Time

IN THE UNITED STATES COURT OF APPEALS
FOR VETERANS CLAIMS

[VETERAN'S NAME],	)	
	)	
Appellant,	)	
	)	
v.	)	[CAVC APPEAL NO.]
	)	
[NAME OF CURRENT SECRETARY],	)	
Secretary of Veterans Affairs,	)	
	)	
Appellee.	)	

APPELLANT'S UNOPPOSED MOTION FOR EXTENSION OF TIME

Pursuant to U.S. Vet. App. Rule 26(b), Appellant, [VETERAN'S NAME], moves the Court for an order extending until the [DAY] day of [MONTH], [YEAR] the time allowed for filing [VETERAN'S NAME]'s [NAME OF PLEADING], presently due on the [DAY] day of [MONTH], [YEAR].

This is Appellant's [NUMBER OF THIS EXTENSION REQUEST] request for an extension of time. The total number of additional days requested by Appellant is [NUMBER OF DAYS REQUESTED] and the total number of additional days previously granted to Appellant in this case is [NUMBER]. Appellee has requested and been granted extensions of time totaling [NUMBER] days **OR** Appellee has not requested any extensions of time in this appeal.

Appellant requests this extension because Appellant needs additional time in order to [REASON (e.g. prepare brief to fully inform Court of issues presented)].

Counsel for Appellee has been consulted and does not object to this motion. **OR** describe effort to contact counsel, e.g., left a message, and state opposing counsel's position is unknown.

Respectfully submitted,

/s/ [E-SIGNATURE]
[NAME]
[FIRM]
[FIRM ADDRESS]
[PHONE NUMBER]

Attorney for Appellant

D. Stay of Appellate Proceedings (Rule 5)

A stay, if granted, of the proceedings suspends appellate proceedings. The court may stay the proceedings on its own initiative or based on motion by a party.

YIELD Do not file a motion for a stay when you really mean to file a motion for an extension, i.e., asking for additional time to file a pleading.

A stay is possible under Rule 5 when

- a motion has been filed with the Board asking it to reconsider or vacate its decision;
- an organization operating under the provisions of Public Law No. 102-229 is conducting a case evaluation; or
- it is otherwise in the interest of judicial efficiency.

If you request a stay to allow the parties time to negotiate a settlement or other joint resolution, the Clerk of Court may stay the case only for a total of 60 days (see the sections above on settlement, remand, and tips on extending time for negotiating). *See* Rule 45 (g)(5). A judge may grant or continue a stay for longer periods.

It is important to know that until the court grants the motion for a stay, just filing the motion does not suspend the proceedings.

After the Stay Expires. After the stay expires, the preexisting briefing schedule resumes at the same point it was stayed. Rule 5(b).

Continuing the Stay. If it is necessary to continue the stay, a party may move for a continuation. As noted above, under Rule 45(g)(5), the Clerk may grant a stay only for a maximum of 60 days when the stay is requested to negotiate a settlement or joint resolution.

A motion to stay the court's proceedings may not be combined with any other motion. The Clerk of Court will return any motion that violates this rule.

E. Important Reminders for Different Types of Motions

1. MOTIONS TO EXPEDITE

Be sure that a Motion to Expedite Proceedings based on a veteran's "serious health condition that makes the death of the veteran or petitioner imminent" is supported with a physician's statement that contains the doctor's licensing authority and current license number. Rule 47(a)(1). *See* the "Expedited Proceedings" section, under "Filing the Notice of Appeal" for more information.

SAMPLE: Joint Motion for a Stay of Proceedings

UNITED STATES COURT OF APPEALS
FOR VETERANS CLAIMS

[VETERAN'S NAME]	)	
	)	
Appellant,	)	
	)	
v.	)	[CAVC APPEAL NO.]
	)	
[NAME OF CURRENT SECRETARY],	)	
Secretary of Veterans Affairs,	)	
	)	
Appellee.	)	

JOINT MOTION FOR A STAY OF PROCEEDINGS

Pursuant to U.S. Vet. App. Rule 5(a)(3) and 45(g)(5), Appellee, [NAME OF CURRENT SECRETARY], Secretary of Veterans Affairs, and Appellant, [VETERAN'S NAME] respectfully move the Court to stay proceedings in the instant case for [NUMBER OF DAYS REQUESTED] days, from [DATE], until [DATE].

As grounds for this motion, the parties submit that they are currently negotiating a possible joint resolution of this case. Therefore, a [NUMBER OF DAYS REQUESTED]-day stay of proceedings is necessary in order to allow the parties to conclude their negotiations and finalize an agreement regarding Appellant's case.

WHEREFORE, Appellee, [NAME OF CURRENT SECRETARY], Secretary of Veterans Affairs, and Appellant, [VETERAN'S NAME], respectfully move the Court to stay proceedings in the instant appeal from [DATE], until [DATE].

Respectfully submitted,

FOR APPELLANT:

/s/ [E-SIGNATURE]
[ATTORNEY'S NAME]
[FIRM]
[ADDRESS]
[PHONE NUMBER]

____
[DATE]

FOR APPELLEE:

[NAME]
General Counsel

[NAME]
Assistant General Counsel

/s/ [E-SIGNATURE]
[ATTORNEY'S NAME]
Deputy Assistant General Counsel

/s/ [E-SIGNATURE]
[ATTORNEY'S NAME]
Appellate Attorney (027)
U.S. Department of Veterans Affairs
810 Vermont Avenue, NW
Washington, DC 20420
Telephone: [PHONE NUMBER]

____
[DATE]

2. MOTIONS DISPUTING THE RBA OR ROP

In a motion disputing the RBA or ROP, be sure to describe the good-faith efforts made to resolve any dispute over the RBA, the ROP, or both. Being able to say that you contacted VA counsel to resolve the dispute will help your case. *See* the section "Record Before the Agency" (Part 4.I) or the section "Record of Proceedings" (Part 5.IV) for more information.

3. MOTIONS FOR LEAVE TO WITHDRAW

Be sure that a Motion for Leave to Withdraw Representation complies with Rule 46(c).

SAMPLE: Motion for Leave to Withdraw

IN THE UNITED STATES COURT OF APPEALS
FOR VETERANS CLAIMS

[VETERAN'S NAME],	)	
	)	
Appellant,	)	
	)	
v.	)	[CAVC APPEAL NO.]
	)	
[NAME OF CURRENT SECRETARY],	)	
Secretary of Veterans Affairs,	)	
	)	
Appellee.	)	

MOTION FOR LEAVE TO WITHDRAW

Pursuant to U.S.Vet. App. Rule 46(d)(4),the undersigned moves the Court for leave to withdraw as counsel for Appellant. In support of this motion the undersigned states:

Appellant's current address is: [CURRENT ADDRESS]

Appellant's current telephone number is: [CURRENT TELEPHONE]

Appellant has been notified that this motion would be filed: and

Copies of all papers filed by the parties, all notices and orders accumulated by the undersigned, and all files belonging to the Appellant have been sent to the client.

Counsel for Appellee has been consulted and does not object to this motion.

Respectfully submitted,

/s/ [E-SIGNATURE]
[NAME]
[FIRM]
[FIRM ADDRESS]
[PHONE NUMBER]

Attorney for Appellant

4. AMENDING A PLEADING

Be sure to file a separate Motion for Leave if you are moving to amend, correct, or supplement a previously filed pleading.

PART 5

The Briefing Process

I. Preparing Your Brief

As detailed in the last part, the Prebriefing Conference affords you the opportunity to present a summary of your argument to the Central Legal Staff (CLS) and VA counsel. If VA counsel is not receptive to your position, however, you will next begin the briefing process.

The CAVC has a specialized set of rules related to all aspects of brief writing, including timing and format. The following sections review the rules governing the briefing process at the CAVC.

A. The Veteran's Opening Brief

You can best serve your client's interests by timely e-filing a properly formatted Opening Brief that includes the required subsections and necessary citations. *See* Rules 31, 32. Where appropriate, you should file a request to seal any brief containing the veteran's protected information, as explained below. Rule 48.

1. TIMING FOR FILING THE VETERAN'S OPENING BRIEF AND EFFECTS OF FAILURE TO FILE (RULE 31)

Rule 31 provides ways to calculate the deadline for a veteran to file an Opening Brief. It also explains what happens if the veteran fails to file the brief on time. This section explains the requirements of Rule 31 and how to obtain an extension of time to file an Opening Brief, if necessary.

a. How to Calculate the Due Date for the Veteran's Opening Brief

Due Date Depends on Dispute of the RBA. The due date for filing a veteran's Opening Brief depends on whether any party disputes the Record Before the Agency (RBA), as set forth in Rule 10(b). *See* Rule 31(a).

If there is no dispute concerning the RBA, the veteran's Opening Brief is due 60 days after the expiration of the 14-day period, plus 5 days for mailing (*see* Rule 26(c), set forth in Rule 10(b) to dispute the RBA).

But, if any party files a motion challenging the RBA, the CAVC will set the due date for filing the veteran's Opening Brief. The Clerk will send an order to each party to the proceeding setting the due date for the veteran's Opening Brief. *See* Rule 45(c).

Notice to File Brief. It is, however, the court's practice to issue a Notice to File Brief to the veteran. Such a notice supersedes the rules, and the Opening Brief will be due 60 days following the date of the Notice. A "day" for the 60-day period includes all calendar days; a "day" is not limited to business days. *See* Rule 26. For example, if the Notice to File Brief is dated January 5, 2012, the first day of the 60-day period is January 6, 2012, and the last day of the 60-day period, i.e., the due date for filing the veteran's Opening Brief, is March 6, 2012:

Example Calculation of Due Date for Filing Veteran's Opening Brief

JANUARY 2012						
SUN	MON	TUE	WED	THU	FRI	SAT
1	2	3	4	5	6	7
8	9	10	11	12	13	14
15	16	17	18	19	20	21
22	23	24	25	26	27	28
29	30	31				

FEBRUARY 2012						
SUN	MON	TUE	WED	THU	FRI	SAT
			1	2	3	4
5	6	7	8	9	10	11
12	13	14	15	16	17	18
19	20	21	22	23	24	25
26	27	28	29			

MARCH 2012						
SUN	MON	TUE	WED	THU	FRI	SAT
				1	2	3
4	5	6	7	8	9	10
11	12	13	14	15	16	17
18	19	20	21	22	23	24
25	26	27	28	29	30	31

End of 60-Day Period Is Not a Business Day. If the 60-day period ends on a Saturday, Sunday, a legal holiday, or any day the court is closed, the due date for filing the veteran's Opening Brief will end on the next court business day. Rule 26(a)(1).

Legal holidays include New Year's Day, Martin Luther King, Jr.'s, Birthday, Presidents' Day, Memorial Day, Independence Day, Labor Day, Columbus Day, Veterans Day, Thanksgiving Day, Christmas Day, and any other day that the President or Congress declares a holiday, such as Inauguration Day. *See* Rule 26(a)(2).

In addition, if the 60-day period ends on a day when the Chief Judge of the CAVC closes the Clerk of Court's Office, or when the Chief Judge declares that the Clerk of Court's Office is inaccessible because of inclement weather or another condition, the due date for filing the veteran's Opening Brief will fall on the next court business day. For example, if the first day of the 60-day period falls on January 10, 2012, the last day of the 60-day period would fall on March 10, 2012, a Saturday. Because the last day of the 60-day period falls on a Saturday, the veteran's Opening Brief would be due on the next business day, Monday, March 12, 2012:

Example Calculation of Due Date for Filing Veteran's Opening Brief

First day of 60-day period

JANUARY 2012						
SUN	MON	TUE	WED	THU	FRI	SAT
1	2	3	4	5	6	7
8	9	10	11	12	13	14
15	16	17	18	19	20	21
22	23	24	25	26	27	28
29	30	31				

FEBRUARY 2012						
SUN	MON	TUE	WED	THU	FRI	SAT
			1	2	3	4
5	6	7	8	9	10	11
12	13	14	15	16	17	18
19	20	21	22	23	24	25
26	27	28	29			

MARCH 2012						
SUN	MON	TUE	WED	THU	FRI	SAT
				1	2	3
4	5	6	7	8	9	10
11	12	13	14	15	16	17
18	19	20	21	22	23	24
25	26	27	28	29	30	31

Due date for filing
the Veteran's Opening Brief

Last day of 60-day period
falling on a Saturday

b. Extending the Time for Filing the Veteran's Opening Brief

If a veteran needs more time to complete the Opening Brief, you may file a Motion for Extension of Time for up to 45 days for good cause. *See* Rule 26(b). Additional time beyond 45 days is granted only for extraordinary circumstances. Rule 26(b).

c. Failure to File the Veteran's Opening Brief

If a veteran fails to file an Opening Brief on time or within the time as extended, the court may take any action it deems appropriate, including dismissing the appeal. Rule 31(b). In addition, VA counsel may move to dismiss the appeal or ask the court to take any other appropriate action. Significantly, the Clerk of Court can dismiss an appeal for a veteran's failure to file an Opening Brief and can act on the Secretary's unopposed motion to dismiss an appeal. *See* Rule 45(g)(1), (h).

The Clerk may grant a consented-to or unopposed motion to reinstate an appeal. Rule 45(g)(1). Additionally, a veteran may ask the Clerk of Court or the court to reconsider dismissal of the case for the failure to file an Opening Brief. Rule 35(a).

2. FORMAT OF THE VETERAN'S OPENING BRIEF (RULE 28)

Rule 28(a) sets forth the format for the veteran's Opening Brief. This format applies to all Opening Briefs except those filed by veterans representing themselves. Veterans who represent themselves may file an informal brief.

For all veterans represented by counsel, however, the veteran's Opening Brief must contain seven sections, in the following order: (a) Table of Contents, (b) Table of Authorities, (c) Statement of Issues, (d) Statement of the Case, (e) Summary of the Argument, (f) Argument, and (g) Conclusion. Additional sections and subsections are not prohibited. This section details the contents of each of the mandatory components of the veteran's Opening Brief as required by Rule 28(a).

SAMPLE: Veteran's Opening Brief Cover

APPELLANT'S BRIEF

UNITED STATES COURT OF APPEALS
FOR VETERANS CLAIMS

No. 00-0000

JOHN Q. VETERAN,

Appellant

v.

______________________________,

SECRETARY OF VETERANS AFFAIRS,

Appellee

Oliver W. Counsel
Lawyer & Lawyer
1111 J Street, NW
Washington, DC 20000
(202) 555-1212

Attorney for Appellant

a. Table of Contents

The Table of Contents lists each section of the Opening Brief (excluding the Table of Contents itself and the title page) and the page on which each section begins.

Although not specifically required by Rule 28(a), because the Argument section is the most complex part of the Opening Brief, the headings and subheadings used in the Argument section should also be listed in the Table of Contents with the corresponding beginning page numbers.

The headings and subheadings are usually done in outline format (e.g., I., A., 1., a., and so forth). Most word-processing software contains tools that will allow you to create a Table of Contents that complies with the requirements of Rule 28(a).

b. Table of Authorities

The Table of Authorities is a table of all legal authorities cited in the Opening Brief. It should first list, in alphabetical order, all cases cited in the brief, along with references to the pages of the brief where the cases are cited. Next, it should list any cited statutes with the page numbers of the brief where the statutes are cited, followed by any other authorities cited in the brief (e.g., treatises, law review articles), along with the page numbers of the brief where these other authorities are cited. The Table of Authorities should then list all regulations and the respective page number where each is cited. Finally, it should list the pages of the RBA cited in the brief, again, with references to the pages of the brief where they are cited. The rules require that if a document in the RBA is composed of more than one page, a citation to a single page in the Table of Authorities must be followed by a parenthetical giving the page range for the complete document. In addition, the rules require a second parenthetical giving a short description of the document cited. See the example table on the next page.

c. Statement of Issues

The Statement of Issues section should include a short introductory statement of the legal issues or points of law involved in the case.

SAMPLE: Table of Authorities for Veteran's Opening Brief

TABLE OF AUTHORITIES

These issues are typically stated in question format and should be phrased in such a way that a "yes" answer will support the veteran's position. The Statement of Issues should be written persuasively for maximum impact. For example: "Did the failure of the Board of Veterans' Appeals to consider and apply 38 C.F.R. § 4.71a, Diagnostic Code 5055, to the facts of this case conflict with the case law of this Court?"

d. Statement of the Case

Although not required by the rules, many practitioners divide the Statement of the Case into at least three sections. These are the Nature of the Case, Course of Proceedings and Disposition Below, and Statement of Facts.

Nature of the Case. This is typically a one- or two-sentence statement explaining the reason for the appeal and what the veteran expects to achieve if he or she prevails.

Course of Proceedings and Disposition Below. This section tells the court how the case began and the procedural steps taken by the parties and the prior tribunals. This generally includes the filing dates of the claims, Notices of Disagreement, and Notices of Appeal. RBA citations should be given to support each statement. This information allows the veteran to establish, and the court to determine on its own, that the court has jurisdiction over the appeal.

Statement of Facts. This section should include all relevant facts pertinent to the issues before the CAVC. Facts should be presented in chronological order and in a persuasive, but not argumentative, manner. Every statement of fact should be supported by a citation to the RBA.

e. Summary of the Argument

The Summary of the Argument section immediately precedes the Argument section. Rule 28(a). This section should briefly summarize each argument, but it should not usually include citations to the RBA or to any legal authorities.

One good way to set up the Summary of the Argument is to begin the first sentence with a statement similar to: "The veteran makes ___ assignments of error." The number that fills in the blank should correspond to the number of issues presented. This is immediately followed by one sentence addressing each issue. This paragraph is concluded by a sentence stating the relief sought. The opening paragraph may be followed by one paragraph addressing, in more detail, each issue to follow. The order of the sentences in the first paragraph and the order of the paragraphs that follow should correspond to the statement of issues at the beginning of the brief.

f. Argument

The Argument section is the core section of the Opening Brief. This section must contain the veteran's contentions on the issues and the reasons for those contentions. Finally, the Argument section should include citations to relevant authorities, such as case law, statutes, and regulations and should also include citations to the RBA, where appropriate. The argument should apply the law, or requested interpretation or extension of law, to the facts. It should analyze why the court should adopt the veteran's argument and rule in his or her favor. Arguments should be presented in the same order as the issues are stated at the beginning of the brief.

g. Conclusion

Rule 28(a) requires every Opening Brief to end with a Conclusion. The Conclusion must state the precise relief sought by the veteran. In many cases, the proper relief will be a reversal on a question of law and an order remanding the appeal to the Board for further proceedings consistent with the court's opinion. This section should be short, generally one paragraph.

h. Other Important Reminders for the Opening Brief

- Motions may not be filed as a substitute for a brief, or incorporated in a brief.
- A Joint Motion for Remand may be filed at any time, even after you have filed the Opening Brief.
- References to the RBA must conform to Rule 10(a).
- Superseded statutes, rules or regulations, or unpublished authorities must be reproduced in relevant part in the brief or in an appendix. An appendix is not required, but if necessary, should be attached to the veteran's Opening Brief (or Reply Brief). An appendix is not the same as the Record of Proceedings (ROP), which is prepared by the Secretary, as explained later.

B. Citation to Certain Authority (Rule 30)

Where to Find CAVC Opinions. You can research CAVC opinions in several locations:

- Legal research engines, e.g., Westlaw and Lexis, contain libraries of CAVC opinions.
- West publishes the Veterans Appeals Reporter.
- The CAVC also places published panel decisions on its website under the "Opinions and Orders" tab. At present, opinions are available as far back as 1989. You can also search the court's website for Decisions and Opinions by going to the "Case Information" tab, selecting "Decisions and Opinions," and entering your search terms.

LexisNexis publishes a CD-ROM in cooperation with the National Veterans Legal Services Program containing CAVC decisions, the complete Veterans Benefits Manual, precedent opinions of the general counsel, the CAVC Rules, and more. Currently, the CD is priced at $206. For more information, search the LexisNexis website for "Veterans Benefits Manual and Related Laws and Regulations on CD-ROM."

Precedential versus Nonprecedential Decisions. The CAVC designates its opinions as precedential and nonprecedential. As a general rule, published decisions of three-judge panels are designated as precedential. Rule 30 forbids citation of a nonprecedential decision unless it has binding or preclusive effect, such as under the "law of the case" doctrine. Thus, it is best to avoid citation of a nonprecedential opinion unless it is for the same veteran you are representing.

The CAVC has authority to strike a noncompliant brief. *See* Bastien v. Shinseki, 599 F.3d 1301, 1307 (Fed. Cir. 2010).

Submission of Supplemental Authority. Rule 30 also provides a mechanism to cite supplemental authority before the court renders its decision.

C. Sealing a Case (Rule 48)

CAVC proceedings are generally required to be open to the public. *See* 38 U.S.C. § 7268(a). But, in some circumstances, all or part of a brief may contain protected information. In these circumstances, the case may be sealed, as discussed in Rule 48.

Situations in Which a Case Qualifies for Sealing by Statute. Examples of cases in which the court may order a brief or ROP sealed include those involving drug abuse, alcoholism or alcohol abuse, infection with HIV/AIDS, or sickle-cell anemia. *See* 38 U.S.C. § 7332.

Other Situations That May Qualify for Sealing. In cases other than those described in 38 U.S.C. § 7332, the court will conduct a balancing test to determine whether the injury alleged by the party seeking to seal a record outweighs the public interest of open judicial proceedings. The court has held that 38 U.S.C. § 7268(a) creates a "presumption of public access" to court records that can be overcome only by a showing of good cause. Stam v. Derwinski, 1 Vet. App. 317 (1991). *Stam* established the requirement that a party seeking to seal a record must articulate "specific facts showing 'clearly defined and serious injury'" if the record becomes public. 1 Vet App. 317 (1991).

How to Seal a Case. To seal a case, you will need to file a Motion to Seal. It is best to file this motion as soon as you determine that sealing is necessary. If the court seals the case, then documents are still listed on the court's docket, but the individual documents cannot be viewed by nonparties, and you will see a small padlock icon next to the docket entry. A representative who logs into the CM/ECF system will be allowed to view the locked documents.

II. The Secretary's Brief

The Secretary is allowed 60 days after service of the veteran's brief to file its brief. Rule 31(a)(2). Unlike in most federal appellate courts, the rules allow the Secretary to make assignments of error even though it is prohibited from filing a Notice of Appeal. The Secretary is directed to include in its brief "any independent assertion of Board error deemed material and relevant to the matters on appeal." Rule 28(b)(2).

III. Veteran's Reply Brief

The veteran has the option to file a Reply Brief, which must be filed no later than 14 days after service of the Secretary's Brief.

The veteran should use the Reply Brief to respond to the Secretary's arguments, especially including any new assignments of error raised by the Secretary.

The Reply Brief is required to have a Table of Authorities, and other sections are optional.

IV. Record of Proceedings (Rule 28.1)

The ROP provides the court with the documents relevant to the appeal and the issues presented. The ROP includes the Board's decision, any document from the RBA cited in a brief, and any other relevant documents.

Secretary Files the ROP. The Secretary has the responsibility to prepare and file the ROP. The Secretary must file the ROP no later than 14 days after the Reply Brief is filed. If no Reply Brief is filed, then the ROP is due 14 days after the last day on which the veteran was entitled to file a reply brief. If the case does not go to full briefing (for example, if it is remanded or settled under an agreement between the parties), then an ROP is never created, filed, or served.

The ROP *only contains* the pages actually cited in the parties' briefs. The cited pages will appear in the ROP bearing the same page numbers as in the RBA and will appear in the same order as in the RBA. Thus, the ROP might appear to be missing pages, when in fact it is not. For example, if the parties' briefs collectively cited pages 27 and 86 (and no pages in between), then the ROP will contain page 27, immediately followed by page 86.

Disputing the Contents of the ROP. If you dispute the contents of the ROP, then the dispute process resembles the dispute process for the RBA. Rule 28.1(b). If your disputes cannot be resolved with VA counsel, then you must file a motion within 14 days after the Secretary files the ROP. The motion must describe your good-faith efforts to resolve any disputes.

V. Oral Argument (Rule 34)

The CAVC rarely holds oral argument. A veteran may request oral argument by filing a motion. The motion for oral argument must be filed no later than 14 days after the Reply Brief is due or filed. The motion must state why argument will aid the court. Rule 34(b). The motion may not be included in a brief.

If the CAVC grants oral argument, the Clerk of Court informs the parties of the date, time, and place for argument. Although argument is almost always held in Washington, D.C., the court may sit anywhere in the United States. Rule 34(a). Parties must arrange in advance with the Clerk to use any demonstratives or other physical evidence other than documents during the argument.

At oral argument, each party is typically allowed 30 minutes. At the hearing, the veteran opens the argument and may reserve time for rebuttal. *See* Rule 34(e). If a party does not appear for the oral argument, the CAVC will hear any other party who is present. Rule 34(f). If oral argument is granted, counsel should *not* merely read the brief.

If the appeal is assigned to a single judge for a decision, oral argument is almost never allowed.

SAMPLE: Veteran's Motion Requesting Oral Argument

IN THE UNITED STATES COURT OF APPEALS
FOR VETERANS CLAIMS

[NAME OF VETERAN]	)	
Appellant,	)	
	)	
v.	)	[CAVC. APPEAL NO.]
	)	
[NAME OF CURRENT SECRETARY],	)	
Secretary of Veterans Affairs,	)	
	)	
Appellee.	)	

APPELLANT'S MOTION
REQUESTING ORAL ARGUMENT

Pursuant to U.S. Vet. App. Rule 34(a), Appellant moves the Court for an Order granting oral argument in the captioned appeal. Appellant filed a reply brief with the Court on [DATE]. This Motion is therefore timely if file on or before [DATE-(14 days after filing the Reply Brief or the Reply Brief was due)].

Argument is appropriate in this case. [STATE WHY ARGUMENT IS APPROPRIATE (e.g., the case presents an issue of first impression, the appellant argues for a modification, extension, or clarification of existing law, etc.)]

Counsel for Appellee has been consulted and has no objection to this motion.

Respectfully submitted,

/s/ [E-SIGNATURE]
[NAME]
[FIRM]
[ADDRESS]
[PHONE NUMBER]

Attorney for Appellant

PART 6

Postbriefing Process

I. The Court's Postbriefing Process

A. Court's Decision-Making Process

As with many federal appellate courts, the CAVC first sends the briefs and ROP to the Court's Central Legal Staff (CLS). Under the court's Internal Operating Procedures, the CLS prepares a memorandum discussing the issues and includes a possible disposition. The Clerk of Court then assigns the appeal to a judge for screening.

Next, the screening judge reviews the appeal and decides whether it warrants a single-judge decision, panel decision, or en banc review. The screening judge will decide the appeal if that judge determines that a single-judge decision is appropriate.

If the screening judge decides that the appeal requires a panel decision (for example, because the case presents a question of first impression), the judge requests that the Clerk create a panel, which will include the screening judge. Senior judges do not participate in panel decisions. The panel then determines whether oral argument will be held.

Finally, the single judge or panel issues the court's decision.

The court usually issues its decision between 6 and 18 months after the court hears oral argument or between 3 and 12 months following the Reply Brief, in the absence of oral argument.

B. Motion for Reconsideration (Rule 35)

Motions for Reconsideration are decided by the same judge or panel that rendered the initial decision.

1. TYPES OF MOTIONS FOR RECONSIDERATION AND ADDITIONAL REVIEW

Following are some common types of Motions for Reconsideration.

Motion for Reconsideration from a Dismissal Under Rule 35. This type of dismissal occurs when a veteran fails to pay the filing fee or file an Opening Brief. Because the Clerk can dismiss an appeal for these reasons, you should first ask the Clerk for reconsideration. Rule 35(a)(1). If the Clerk denies that motion, the matter will automatically be referred to a judge.

Motion for Reconsideration from Decision of a Single Judge. If your case was decided by a single judge, then you may move for reconsideration by the same single judge. But, you may file only one Motion for Reconsideration. In other words, if your Motion for Reconsideration by the same single judge is denied, you may file a motion for a panel decision, but you may not file a second motion for single-judge reconsideration.

Motion for Panel Decision. If your case was decided by a single judge, you may also move for a decision by a panel without first seeking single-judge reconsideration. Rule 35(b). The court will convene a panel of three judges, including the author of the single-judge decision, to consider your motion for a panel decision.

In your Motion for Reconsideration, you may ask for both single-judge reconsideration and, if reconsideration is denied, a panel decision. Rule 35(a)(1).

Motion for Full-Court Review. If your appeal was decided and denied by a panel, then you may move for a decision by the full court. Should your request be denied, you may not file a Motion for Reconsideration of that decision. Rule 35(a)(2)(C).

If a case was decided by a single judge, a party may not move directly for a decision by the full court. Rather, the party must first move for a decision by a panel. Rule 35(c)(1). Full-court decisions are reserved for exceptional cases.

---

2. TIME FOR FILING ALL MOTIONS FOR RECONSIDERATION

All Motions for Reconsideration, panel review, or full-court review must be filed no later than 21 days after the date of the first dispositive action. A motion for single-judge reconsideration may be combined with a motion for panel review. Likewise, a motion for panel reconsideration may be combined with a motion for full-court review. Rule 35(d).

To be timely under the Rules, any Motion for Reconsideration, panel review, or full-court review must be filed within the 21-day filing period.

---

3. CONTENTS OF THE MOTION FOR RECONSIDERATION

The Motion for Reconsideration must state the points of law or fact that the party believes the court has overlooked or misunderstood. The motion may not exceed 15 pages without the court's permission. It must otherwise comply with Rule 27 but need not indicate whether it is opposed. Rule 35(f).

4. RESPONSE TO ANY MOTIONS FOR RECONSIDERATION

The nonmoving party may file a response to a Motion for Reconsideration only if one is requested by the court. Rule 35(g).

C. Entry of Judgment (Rule 36)

The court will enter judgment on the docket after the later of (1) the date on which the 21-day time period for filing a Motion for

Reconsideration has expired or (2) the date on which the court denies the last pending Motion for Reconsideration under Rule 35.

Entry of judgment begins the 60-day time period for any appeal to the United States Court of Appeals for the Federal Circuit (CAFC).

SAMPLE ORDER: CAVC Judgment

Not Published

UNITED STATES COURT OF APPEALS FOR VETERANS CLAIMS

NO:

, APPELLANT,

V.

ERIC K. SHINSEKI,
SECRETARY OF VETERANS AFFAIRS, APPELLEE.

JUDGMENT

The Court has issued a decision in this case. The time allowed for motions under Rule 35 of the Court's Rules of Practice and Procedure has expired.

Under Rule 36, judgment is entered this date.

Dated: August 23, 2011

FOR THE COURT:

GREGORY O. BLOCK
Clerk of the Court

By: /s/ Joan E. Sayers
Deputy Clerk

Copies to:

[redacted]

[redacted]

VA General Counsel (027)

D. Issuance of Mandate (Rule 41)

The "mandate" of the court is executed by the Clerk of Court as a ministerial action. The mandate is evidence that a judgment has become final and directs the Board or Secretary to take the actions required by the court's decision.

Mandate Following a Decision of the Court. In the case of a decision by a panel or a single judge, the mandate will generally issue no earlier than 60 days after the date of the entry of judgment under Rule 36.

Mandate Following a Joint Motion for Remand. Where the parties file a Joint Motion for Remand, however, the court's order granting the joint motion constitutes the judgment and mandate because of the consensual nature of the joint motion. *See* Bowers v. Brown, 8 Vet. App. 25, 27 (1995).

Mandate Following Appeal to Higher Court. If a timely Notice of Appeal to the CAFC is filed with the CAVC Clerk, the mandate of the CAVC will issue in accordance with 38 U.S.C. § 7291(a) (governing the rules for issuing CAVC mandates following decisions of the CAFC and/or the U.S. Supreme Court).

II. Applications for Attorneys' Fees Under the Equal Access to Justice Act (EAJA) (Rule 39)

A. What Is EAJA?

Congress enacted the EAJA in 1948 (5 U.S.C. § 504; 28 U.S.C. § 2412). In the context of veterans' appeals, the EAJA is a fee-shifting statute that provides for the award of attorneys' fees and other expenses (including filing fees) to eligible veterans who are parties to litigation against the government. Ardestani v. INS, 502 U.S. 129 (1991).

To be eligible, the veteran must prevail over the government. Fees and expenses will nonetheless not be awarded if the court finds that the Secretary's position was "substantially justified" or there are other special circumstances making an award unjust. The "Secretary's position" includes the position taken by the government in the litigation, as well as the position adopted by the VA in the administrative proceedings. 28 U.S.C. § 2412(d)(2)(D).

SAMPLE ORDER: CAVC Mandate

Not Published

UNITED STATES COURT OF APPEALS FOR VETERANS CLAIMS

NO:

, APPELLANT,

V.

ERIC K. SHINSEKI,
SECRETARY OF VETERANS AFFAIRS, APPELLEE.

MANDATE

The time for reconsideration, review, or appeal of the Court's decision has expired. That decision is final and is not subject to further review.

Under Rule 41(a) of the Court's Rules of Practice and Procedure, mandate is effective October 24, 2011.

Dated: October 25, 2011

FOR THE COURT:

GREGORY O. BLOCK
Clerk of the Court

By: /s/ Joan E. Sayers
Deputy Clerk

Copies to:

[redacted]

A party has "prevailed" when he or she has been successful on any significant issue in the case that achieves some of the benefits the party sought. The lawsuit must be the material factor in bringing about the desired result, not a gratuitous act by the government. *See* Buckhannon Bd. & Care Home, Inc. v. W. Va. Dep't of Health & Human Res., 532 U.S. 598 (2001) (rejecting catalyst theory).

Generally, an award from an EAJA claim reduces the amount of fees owed by the veteran to his attorney. The EAJA award may or may not cover all of the attorneys' fees and expenses, and, depending on the engagement or fee agreement, the veteran may owe the remainder of the attorneys' fees. Appellants are entitled only to fees and expenses associated with the issues on which they prevailed.

B. Why Does the Government Pay for Me to Do This Work?

Congress enacted the Equal Access to Justice Act (EAJA) in 1948 after finding that individuals and others may be deterred from seeking review of, or defending against, unreasonable governmental action because of the expense involved. *See* H.R. Rep. No. 96-1418 (1980), *reprinted in* 1980 U.S.C.C.A.N. 4984. Congress hoped that the EAJA would encourage civil action providing a concrete, adversarial test of the government regulation, ensuring the legitimacy and fairness of the law. S. Rep. No. 96-253, at 5–6 (1979), *reprinted in* 1980 U.S.C.C.A.N. 4953, 4988–89.

C. What Types of Cases Qualify for an EAJA Award?

Some common examples of situations where EAJA fees have been awarded include:

- **Joint Motion for Remand**. The veteran and VA agree to a Joint Motion for Remand (on at least one issue in the case due to administrative error[1]) sending the case back to the Board.

1. In this context, an administrative error means that, for example, the Board neglected to give reasons or bases for its finding or failed to apply the correct law. If a remand was based on, for example, an intervening change in the law after the Board made its initial decision, then such an error would not be an administrative error. In the latter case, the veteran would not qualify to apply for an EAJA award.

- **Settlement.** The VA agrees to settle one or more of the claims brought by the veteran.
- **Reversal of the Board.** The CAVC vacates the Board's decision and remands one or more of the issues brought by the veteran to the Board.
- **Preparation of Application.** Fees are available for work preparing the fee application.

When applying for EAJA based on a Joint Motion for Remand citing an administrative error, it is important that the Motion clearly establish the administrative error. It may be sufficient if the Motion includes language such as "the Board did not" or "the Board erred." The VA may object to phrases such as "the Board failed." Any court order vacating a Board decision and remanding an appeal at least implies prejudicial error.

D. How Do I Calculate Qualifying Fees and Expenses?

1. ATTORNEYS' FEES

Generally, EAJA fees are limited to $125 per hour, without some justification for a higher fee. *See* Baldi Bros. Constructors v. United States, 52 Fed. Cl. 78 (2002).

Justification for Higher Attorneys' Fees. Justification for a higher fee is supported in areas with a higher cost of living, which allows for the EAJA fee to increase by a factor tied to the Consumer Price Index (CPI).

The CPI factor can be found by searching the Bureau of Labor Statistics website online at http://www.bls.gov/. Select "Subject Areas," then "Consumer Price Indexes," followed by "CPI Databases." On the "Databases," screen select "Top Picks" on the first row titled "All Urban Consumers." Place a check mark in the box for your area and press "Retrieve data." The CPI is not published every month for all areas. The CPI factor is usually expressed by a number in the hundreds. For example, the CPI factor for Washington, D.C., in May 2012 was 150.155.

To determine the appropriate CPI rate, use the CPI rate for the month the veteran's Opening Brief or Joint Motion for Remand was filed, and apply this rate for all work performed during the appeal. If that date falls between two of the months that the CPI is published, use the rate for the earlier month. In other words, if you filed the veteran's Opening Brief in February, use the CPI factor published in January.

Calculating Higher Attorneys' Fee Rates. To calculate the higher hourly rate for the Washington, D.C., area, use the following formula:

$$\text{Higher hourly rate} = \$125\ (\text{standard rate}) \times \frac{\text{CPI factor}}{100}$$

For example, using the May 2012 CPI factor for Washington, D.C., an attorney could use $187.69 as the hourly rate in an EAJA application for an appeal where the veteran's Opening Brief was filed in May 2012.

In other areas, the formula is:

$$\text{Higher hourly rate} = \$125\ (\text{standard rate}) \times \frac{\text{CPI factor}}{\text{CPI for March 1996}}$$

2. PARALEGAL HOURLY RATES

Fees for work performed by nonattorneys included on the EAJA application should be at a rate less than the $125/hour statutory rate, with $90/hour being a reasonable amount unlikely to be challenged by the VA. The education and other qualifications of the nonattorneys to perform the work they were assigned should be stated in the affidavit of lead counsel, which must support the fee application. Rule 39(f).

3. EXPENSES

Expenses may include filing fees; bills for electronic legal research; travel related to the appeal (e.g., mileage or airfare to review the original administrative record in Washington, D.C., or the virtual record at your local Regional Office, or for oral argument); postage; and photocopying.

Time spent on Motions for Extension of Time (due to your own obligations, not attributable to VA conduct) and work by secretaries do not qualify for reimbursement under the EAJA.

E. Preparing the EAJA Application

Under Rule 39, a written application must be filed no later than 30 days after the court's judgment becomes final under 38 U.S.C. § 7291(a). The judgment generally becomes final 90 days after it is issued, except when the case is appealed to the Federal Circuit.

Your request may not exceed 20 pages, not including appendix pages. You must attach to your application an affidavit by lead counsel. That affidavit must include a description of the qualifications for any nonattorney and, if the veteran paid the filing fee, an affidavit from the veteran establishing that his or her net worth was less than $2 million on the day the appeal was filed. This affidavit is not required to be notarized. The application must also be supported by an itemized bill for all other expenses.

The deadline to file an EAJA application is *not* extendible.

Affidavit by the Lead Counsel. The affidavit must include a chronological list of all time expended by all lawyers and nonlawyers, such as paralegals. You may claim fees for the time spent preparing the EAJA application and supporting materials. This affidavit does not need to be notarized.

The affidavit must include an itemized statement reporting the actual time expended and the rate at which fees and other expenses were computed. 28 U.S.C. § 2412(d)(1)(B). The statement should show the amount of time you are including in the EAJA application and the amount of time you are deducting, if any. You should consider deducting excessive time spent on a particular task (e.g., an above-average amount of time spent on legal research or drafting/revising your Opening Brief). Also, avoid time entries for blocks of time greater than three hours. Break up the individual tasks into smaller increments of less than three hours to reduce the likelihood that the VA will contest a time entry or that the CAVC will find the amount of time for which fees are claimed to be unreasonable.

Qualifications for Any Nonattorney. A description of the qualifications for any nonattorney (e.g., legal assistant, law student) should be included.

Other Expenses. Other expenses, such as legal research costs (including access to research databases), may also be included in the EAJA application. An itemized bill for the legal research costs should be attached to or included in the EAJA application.

STOP The deadline to file an EAJA application depends on whether the appeal was concluded by a joint disposition filed by the parties or a CAVC decision, either single-judge or panel. If, for example, the CAVC granted a Joint Motion for Remand, then the fee application must be filed within 30 days of the order granting the Joint Motion. If, however, the appeal was resolved by a CAVC decision, then the 30-day period for filing the fee application runs from the date that decision becomes final. See below.

F. Secretary's Response and Your Reply

Secretary's Response. After you file the application, the government files a response within 30 days.

Veteran's Reply. Within 30 days after the government's response, you may file an optional reply to the response.

Effect of Appeal to a Higher Court. If either party timely appeals to the Federal Circuit or the Supreme Court, the court's judgment will not issue until those proceedings are completed; thus, your EAJA application will not be due until after those appeals have run their course and the CAVC's decision becomes final. *See* Rule 39(b)(3).

G. Agreement on Attorneys' Fees and Expenses After Your EAJA Application Is Filed

In many cases, after you file your EAJA application, VA counsel will contact you and offer a compromise amount to settle the EAJA fee claim. Depending on your engagement or fee agreement, if your client has retained the right to agree to the EAJA settlement, then consult your client before agreeing to any compromise amount.

If the parties have agreed on a compromise amount, the Secretary will generally file a response to the application indicating the agreed compromise amount. If the veteran does not file a reply disputing the compromise reported by the Secretary, the court will issue an order awarding fees in the amount reported by the Secretary.

YIELD

EAJA fee applications must include the appeal or petition case number as part of the file name. For instance, if the case number is 12-9999, then the EAJA application file name should be "12-9999 EAJA Fee Application."

H. How Long Does It Take to Get My Check?

If your application is not contested by the VA, the CAVC will issue an order awarding the EAJA fees in approximately 14 days or fewer. After the court's order, it can take from 60 to 90 days to receive payment for the fees awarded.

If your application is contested by the VA, that process could add an additional 60 to 90 days (making the total time to receive fees included in the EAJA application 120 to 180 days).

If you have not received a check within 90 days after the court order granting your EAJA fee application, you should contact VA counsel to inquire about the status. Delays or problems in receiving payment from an approved EAJA application could be solved by filing a Petition for a Writ of Mandamus as a last resort.

III. Appealing to the Court of Appeals for the Federal Circuit

The Court of Appeals for the Federal Circuit (CAFC or Federal Circuit) has exclusive appellate jurisdiction over all appeals from decisions of the CAVC. *See* 38 U.S.C. § 7292(c). Once a practitioner receives an adverse decision from the CAVC, an appeal lies by right to the Federal Circuit. The judgment of the Federal Circuit in the matter is final, subject only to review on a Petition for Certiorari to the Supreme Court.

A. Limitations on Jurisdiction

The Federal Circuit has limited appellate jurisdiction over decisions of the CAVC. In deciding whether to appeal to the Federal Circuit, the practitioner should carefully consider whether the Federal Circuit has jurisdiction over the subject matter of the proposed appeal.

The Federal Circuit has jurisdiction to review and decide any challenge to the validity of any statute or regulation, or any interpretation of it under 38 U.S.C. § 7292, and to interpret constitutional and statutory provisions, other than the disability rating schedule, to the extent presented, relied on in the CAVC decision and necessary to the CAVC decision. 38 U.S.C. § 7292(c), (d). If the issue to be appealed satisfies these criteria, the Federal Circuit may "decide all relevant questions of law, including interpreting constitutional and statutory provisions." 38 U.S.C. § 7292(d). Further, the Federal Circuit also has jurisdiction to review any regulations and interpretations thereof and must hold unlawful and set aside any regulation or any interpretation thereof that is contrary to law. *See* 38 U.S.C. § 7292(d)(1). The Federal Circuit, however, explicitly lacks jurisdiction to review

1. a challenge to a factual determination; or
2. a challenge to a law or regulation as applied to the facts of a particular case.

38 U.S.C. § 7292(d)(2).

B. Notice of Appeal to the Federal Circuit

The first step in appealing a decision of the CAVC to the Federal Circuit is filing a written Notice of Appeal to the Federal Circuit with the CAVC. A Notice of Appeal may be filed at the CAVC by any of the means previously discussed.

The Notice of Appeal to the Federal Circuit must be filed with the CAVC, not the Federal Circuit.

The Notice of Appeal to the Federal Circuit must

1. specify the party or parties taking the appeal by naming each one in the caption or body of the notice;
2. designate the judgment, order, or part thereof being appealed; and
3. name the Federal Circuit as the court to which the appeal is being taken.

See Fed. R. App. P. 3(c).

Because the United States (i.e., the Secretary of Veterans Affairs) is a party in these types of appeals, a Notice of Appeal must be filed within 60 days after the CAVC's judgment in the case or its entry of the order being appealed. Fed. R. App. P. 4(a)(2); 38 U.S.C. § 7292(a). *See* the "Entry of Judgment" section for more information.

The time period for filing a Notice of Appeal to the Federal Circuit is set by CAFC rule and therefore may be extended. Such extensions are unusual.

Once the Notice of Appeal has been received by the CAVC, the Clerk will transmit the Notice and other information about the appeal to the Clerk of Court for the Federal Circuit. The Federal Circuit will then issue a Notice of Docketing, which officially begins the Federal Circuit appeal.

As with appeals to the CAVC, you should keep evidence of the date you sent the Notice of Appeal to the Federal Circuit to the CAVC.

Form: Notice of Appeal to the Federal Circuit

IN THE UNITED STATES COURT OF APPEALS
FOR VETERANS CLAIMS

[VETERAN'S NAME],	)	
	)	
Appellant,	)	
	)	
v.	)	[CAVC APPEAL NO.]
	)	
[NAME OF CURRENT SECRETARY],	)	
Secretary of Veterans Affairs,	)	
	)	
Appellee.	)	

NOTICE OF APPEAL

Notice is hereby given that [VETERAN'S NAME], Appellant, appeals to the United States Court of Appeals for the Federal Circuit from this Court's [DATE], judgment in the captioned appeal.

Respectfully submitted,

/s/ [E-SIGNATURE]
[NAME]
[FIRM]
[ADDRESS]
[PHONE NUMBER]

Attorney for Appellant

C. Federal Circuit Rules of Practice

Practice before the Federal Circuit is governed by the Federal Rules of Appellate Procedure and by the Rules of Practice for the Court of Appeals for the Federal Circuit. These rules may be downloaded from the CAFC website.[2]

D. Admission to the Federal Circuit

The next step in the appeal process is getting admitted to the bar of the Federal Circuit. An attorney is eligible for admission to the bar of the Federal Circuit if that attorney is of good moral and professional character and is admitted to practice before, and of good standing in, various tribunals, including the CAVC.

An attorney may be admitted to the bar of the Federal Circuit by motion in open court, motion by an attorney already admitted to the bar of the Federal Circuit, or upon his or her own motion. Consult CAFC Rule 46 for the procedures to become admitted to the bar of the Federal Circuit.

As of the time of this writing, the fee for admission to the bar of the Federal Circuit is $50.00, in addition to the Judicial Conference fee of $150.00, payable to the CAFC Clerk of Court. *See* CAFC Rule 46(c).

E. Getting Help for Cases Heading to the Federal Circuit

Advice or assistance with an appeal to the CAFC may be available. Consult the Federal Circuit Bar Association, the National Veterans Legal Services Program, or similar nonprofit organizations. Assistance may include a possible referral to volunteer attorney advisors with experience in the Federal Circuit who might be willing to assist you.

2. http://www.cafc.uscourts.gov/.

APPENDICES

Department of Veterans Affairs Acronyms and Abbreviations

ACDUTRA	Active duty for training
AD	Active duty; or right ear
AMC	Appeals Management Center
AO	Agent Orange
AS	Left ear
BD	Board of Veterans' Appeals' Decision
Board	Board of Veterans' Appeals
BVA	Board of Veterans' Appeals
CAD	Coronary artery disease
CAFC	United States Court of Appeals for the Federal Circuit
CAVC	United States Court of Appeals for Veterans Claims
C.F.R.	Code of Federal Regulations
CHF	Congestive heart failure
CIB	Combat Infantryman Badge
C/L	Conclusion of Law
CM/ECF	Case Management/Electronic Case Files
court	United States Court of Appeals for Veterans Claims
COPD	Chronic obstructive pulmonary disease
CPI	Consumer Price Index
CVA	Cerebrovascular accident (stroke)
DAV	Disabled American Veterans
DC	Diagnostic Code

DFH	Declaration of Financial Hardship
DIC	Dependency and Indemnity Compensation
DM	Diabetes mellitus
DSM	American Psychiatric Association, Diagnostic and Statistical Manual of Mental Disorders
EAJA	Equal Access to Justice Act
EED	Earlier effective date
EKG	Electrocardiogram
F/F	Finding of fact
FR	Federal Register
GAF	Global Assessment of Functioning; found in the DSM
GERD	Gastroesophageal reflux disease
GSW	Gunshot wound
HHD	Hypertensive heart disease
HPT	Hypertension
HVD	Hypertensive vascular disease
INACDUTRA	Inactive duty training
IME	Independent medical examination, independent medical expert, or independent medical expert opinion
IR	Increased rating
JMR	Joint Motion for Remand
JMS	Joint Motion for Stay of Proceedings
KC	Korean Conflict
LLE/LUE	Left lower extremity; left upper extremity
LOD	Line of duty
LOM	Limitation of motion
LS	Lumbosacral or lumbar spine
LVH	Left ventricular hypertrophy
MET	Motion for Extension of Time
MG	Muscle Group
MI	Myocardial infarction (heart attack)
NOA	Notice of Appeal
NOD	Notice of Disagreement

NSC	Non (or not) service connected
NSO	National Service Officer
OGC	Office of General Counsel
OSA	Obstructive sleep apnea
PA	Physician's Assistant
PAD	Peripheral arterial disease
PBC	Prebriefing Conference
PFS	Prepared, filed, and served
PFT	Pulmonary function test (or testing)
PH	Purple Heart
PNOA	Protective Notice of Appeal
P&T	Permanent and total (or permanently and totally) disabled
PTSD	Post-traumatic stress disorder
PVD	Peripheral vascular disease
RBA	Record Before the Agency
RFB	Retained foreign body
RLE/RUE	Right lower extremity; right upper extremity
RO	VA Regional Office
ROM	Range of motion
ROP	Record of Proceedings
SC	Service connection or service connected
Secretary	Secretary of Veterans Affairs
SFW	Shell fragment wound
SMC	Special monthly compensation
SMR(s)	Service medical record(s)
SNHL	Sensorineural hearing loss
SOC	Statement of the Case
SSOC	Supplemental Statement of the Case
STR(s)	Service treatment record(s)
TBI	Traumatic brain injury
TDIU	Total disability rating based on individual unemployability
V	Veteran
VA	Department of Veterans Affairs

VAMC	Department of Veterans Affairs Medical Center
VAOPGCPREC	Precedent Opinion by the VA Office of General Counsel
VE	Vietnam Era
VLJ	Veterans Law Judge, i.e., member of the Board of Veterans' Appeals
WIA	Wounded in action

Sample Memorandums

Prebriefing Conference Memorandum

MEMORANDUM

TO: Central Legal Staff, U.S. Court of Appeals for Veterans Claims
[INSERT NAME], Appellate Counsel, U.S. Dept. of Veterans Affairs

FROM: [ATTORNEY NAME], [ATTORNEY'S FIRM]
Attorney for [Appellant]

SUBJECT: CAVC Appeal No. [APPEAL NUMBER]

DATE: [DATE]

The Court issued an order on [DATE OF ORDER], scheduling a telephonic briefing conference in the subject appeal for [TIME OF CONFERENCE] on [DATE OF CONFERENCE]. The order requires the undersigned to submit a summary of the issues [NAME OF APPELLANT] intends to raise on appeal, along with citations to the relevant authorities and the record. This memorandum responds to the Court's order.

I. Background

Appellant ("[NAME OF APPELLANT]" or "Veteran") served on active duty from April 1967 to April 1969 as a tank mechanic in the Army. R. 4, 174. While on active duty, he sustained a back injury when he fell off a tank. R. 174. The Veteran has service connection and a twenty-percent (20%) rating for degenerative changes of the lumbar spine effective December 30, 2005, which was increased to forty percent (40%) effective June 10, 2009. R. 18, 75.

This case arises from a September 19, 2011, decision by the Board of Veterans' Appeal ("Board"), which in turn, was an appeal of a November 2006, Regional Office ("RO") decision. In the 2006 RO decision, the Department of Veterans Affairs granted

[NAME OF APPELLANT] service connection for a low-back disability and assigned a twenty-percent rating effective on December 20, 2005. *See* R. 1267. On appeal to the Board, the case was remanded for additional evidentiary development.

II. The Board's Decision

In the decision being appealed, the Board held that "a higher rating of 40 percent for the orthopedic manifestations of the service-connected low back disability is found to be warranted beginning on June 10, 2009, when the disability picture was first shown to have more nearly approximated that of forward flexion of the thoracolumbar spine restricted to at least 30 degrees." R. 16. The Board thus denied a rating of higher than twenty percent (20%) for the orthopedic manifestations of the low-back disability prior to June 10, 2009. *Id.* The Board based its decision to deny an initial rating of forty percent (40%) on findings from two examinations of the Veteran and other treatment records. R. 10-11. An October 2005 MRI "revealed right L5/S1 disc extrusion and nerve compression and moderate generalized degenerative spondylosis." R. 10. A November 2006 treatment record . . . .

III. Appellant's Arguments

[NAME OF APPELLANT] will argue for reversal of the Board's decision denying an initial rating in excess of twenty-percent (20%) for degenerative changes of his lumbar spine prior to June 10, 2009, or alternatively that remand is required because the Board's statement of reasons or bases is inadequate for judicial review.

First, [NAME OF VETERAN] will argue that the Board committed prejudicial, legal error when it failed to grant an increased rating from 20 to 40 percent prior to June

10, 2009, for the orthopedic manifestations of the service-connected degenerative changes in his lumbar spine. [NAME OF VETERAN] will argue that the medical evidence demonstrates that he had functional loss of forward flexion to less than 30 degrees and the Board provided inadequate reasons or bases as it failed to consider functional loss due to pain.

The VA disability rating schedule provides that a disability rating of twenty percent (20%) applies to "[f]orward flexion of the thoracolumbar spine greater than 30 degrees but not greater than 60 degrees. . . ." 38 C.F.R. § 4.71a (General Rating Formula for Diseases and Injuries of the Spine). The schedule further provides that a disability rating of forty percent (40%) applies to "forward flexion of the thoracolumbar spine 30 degrees or less." *Id.* "While pain alone does not constitute a functional loss under VA regulations that evaluate disability based upon range-of-motion loss," the Board may not deny a claim based on a VA medical examination "that did not adequately address whether the pain resulted in a functional loss. . . ." *See Mitchell v. Shinseki*, 25 Vet. App. 32, 33, 43-44 (2011).

The record includes evidence of neurological manifestations consistent with moderate impairment for the right-lower extremity. *See, e.g.*, R. 463 ("visible" right-lower extremity atrophy); R. 175 (weakness in both lower extremities); R. 845, 1173, 1187, 1200, 1271. [NAME OF VETERAN] will argue, however, that the Board ignored this evidence. Instead, the Board merely stated

> the record does not show that a rating in excess of 10 percent is warranted for the right lower extremity as the findings do not equate with more than mild incomplete paralysis. . . . The January 2010 VA examination, which

> confirmed radiculopathy and neurological deficits, only reflects mild impairment involving the right lower extremity as sensation was noted to be intact.

R. 17. The Board's findings are conclusory and inadequate on their face. *See Dennis v. Nicholson*, 21 Vet. App. 18, 22 (2007); *Abernathy v. Principi*, 3 Vet. App. 461, 465 (1992). [NAME OF VETERAN] will argue that intact sensation does not limit a veteran to a 10-percent rating, that proper consideration of the record as a whole warrants a twenty-percent (20%) rating for his right-lower extremity, and the Board provided inadequate reasons or bases for denying such a rating.

IV. Conclusion

The Court should vacate the Board's decision and remand the appeal with instructions to conduct further proceedings consistent with the Court's order.

/s/
ATTORNEY
[Firm Name]
[Address]

[Phone Number]

Attorney for Appellant

Joint Motion for Remand

IN THE UNITED STATES COURT OF APPEALS
FOR VETERANS CLAIMS

[NAME OF APPELLANT],	)	
	)	
Appellant,	)	
	)	
v.	)	Vet. App. No. [APPEAL NUMBER]
	)	
[NAME OF CURRENT SECRETARY],	)	
Secretary of Veterans Affairs,	)	
	)	
Appellee.	)	

JOINT MOTION FOR REMAND

Pursuant to U.S. Vet. App. R. 27(a) and 45(g), the parties, through their respective counsel, respectfully move this Court to issue an Order vacating the [DATE OF BOARD DECISION], decision of the Board of Veterans' Appeals ("Board" or "BVA") that denied entitlement to benefits under 38 U.S.C. § 1151 for left-knee instability, status post total-knee arthroplasty ("TKA") performed at the ___________ VA Medical Center ("VAMC") on March 6, 2003. The parties move the Court to remand the appeal for readjudication. For the purposes of this Motion only, the parties accept the facts as presented in the BVA decision, unless otherwise noted.

BASIS FOR REMAND

The parties agree that vacatur and remand are required because the Board failed to provide an adequate statement of reasons or bases for its decision. *See* 38 U.S.C. § 7104(d)(1); *Gilbert v. Derwinski*, 1 Vet. App. 49, 57 (1990). Specifically, the Board did not adequately consider whether Appellant had been fully informed as to the potential risks associated with the TKA, thereby preventing Appellant from giving full and informed consent as required by 38 C.F.R. § 17.32(b).

The statute presently provides:

> (a) Compensation . . . shall be awarded for qualifying additional disability . . . in the same manner as if such disability . . . were service-connected. For the purposes of this section, a disability . . . is a qualifying additional disability . . . if the disability . . . was not the result of misconduct and-
>
> (1) the disability . . . was caused by hospital care, medical or surgical treatment, or examination furnished the veteran under any law administered by the Secretary . . . and the proximate cause of the disability or death was-
>
> (A) carelessness, negligence, lack of proper skill, error in judgment, or similar instance of fault on the part of the Department in furnishing the hospital care, medical or surgical treatment, or examination; or
>
> (B) an event not reasonably foreseeable.

38 U.S.C. § 1151.

The law requires the VA to obtain a patient's full and informed consent. The governing statute provides that all patient care administered by the VA "shall be carried out only with the full and informed consent of the patient . . . ." 38 U.S.C. § 7331.

Under the VA regulation implementing § 7331, 38 C.F.R. § 3.361(d)(1)(ii), negligence, error in judgment, or "similar instances of fault" may be found when medical treatment is carried out "without the [V]eteran's . . . informed consent." *See also* 38 C.F.R. § 17.32(b) (2011). For informed consent to be adequately given, the practitioner administering the medical treatment must explain, *inter alia*, the "reasonably foreseeable associated risks" of the treatment. 38 C.F.R. § 17.32(c). Furthermore, "[t]he informed consent process must be appropriately documented in the medical record." 38 C.F.R. § 17.32(d). Appropriate documentation requires signature consent in any case where anesthesia is to be administered.

In denying Appellant entitlement to compensation for the left-knee instability, status post-TKA performed at the _______________, VAMC on March 6, 2003, the Board found that, prior to the procedure in question, the risks and benefits of a TKA were discussed at length, after which she expressed her desire to undergo the procedure and her informed consent to proceed with the surgery was obtained. [R. at 12]. Given that the issue on appeal specifically deals with left-knee instability resulting from her TKA, the Board's lack of a discussion regarding whether instability was addressed in the pre-operative discussion or if not, whether it should have been explicitly listed as a reasonably foreseeable associated risk of the procedure, is not supported by an adequate statement of reasons or bases, frustrating judicial review and requiring vacatur and remand. *See* 38 C.F.R. § 17.32(c), (d); *Gilbert,* 1 Vet. App. at 57.

CONCLUSION

The parties respectfully move the Court to issue an Order vacating the [DATE], Board decision that denied entitlement to VA compensation pursuant to 38 U.S.C. 1151 for left-knee instability, status post-TKA performed at the _______________, VAMC on [DATE]. Appellant is entitled to submit additional evidence and argument during the remand proceedings, *Kutscherousky v. West*, 12 Vet. App. 369, 372 (1999), and VA is obligated to conduct a critical examination of the justification for the decision, *Fletcher v. Derwinski*, 1 Vet. App. 394, 397 (1991). In any subsequent decision, the Board must set forth adequate reasons or bases for its findings and conclusions on all material issues of fact and law presented on the record. 38 U.S.C. § 7104(d)(1). The Board shall also incorporate copies of the Court's order and this motion into Appellant's claims file. Finally, the Secretary "shall take such actions as may be necessary to provide for the expeditious treatment" of this claim. 38 U.S.C. § 7112. The Court should remand the appeal to the Board for further proceedings in accordance with the Court's order and this joint motion.

Respectfully submitted,
FOR THE APPELLANT:

/s/ [e-signature]
[Attorney's Name]
[Firm Names]
[Firm Address]

[Phone Number]

FOR THE APPELLEE:

[Name]
General Counsel

[Name]
Assistant General Counsel

/s/ [e-signature]
[Name]
Deputy Assistant General Counsel

/s/ [e-signature of working attorney]
[Name]
Appellate Attorney
Office of the General Counsel (027)
U.S. Dept. of Veterans Affairs
810 Vermont Avenue, N.W.
Washington, D.C. 20420
[Phone Number]

Index